Practical prescribing for musculoskeletal practitioners

Practical prescribing for musculoskeletal practitioners

Julie Dawson
and
Sheena Hennell

PRACTICAL PRESCRIBING FOR MUSCULOSKELETAL PRACTITIONERS
Julie Dawson and Sheena Hennell
ISBN: 978-1-905539-09-3

First published 2007

British Library Catalogue in Publication Data
A catalogue record for this book is available from the British Library

Notice
Clinical practice and medical knowledge constantly evolve. Standard safety precautions must be followed, but, as knowledge is broadened by research, changes in practice, treatment and drug therapy may become necessary or appropriate. Readers must check the most current product information provided by the manufacturer of each drug to be administered and verify the dosages and correct administration, as well as contraindications. It is the responsibility of the practitioner, utilising the experience and knowledge of the patient, to determine dosages and the best treatment for each individual patient. Any brands mentioned in this book are as examples only and are not endorsed by the Publisher. Neither the publisher nor the authors assume any liability for any injury and/or damage to persons or property arising from this publication.

The Publisher
To contact M&K Publishing write to:
M&K Update Ltd · The Old Bakery · St. John's Street · Keswick · Cumbria CA12 5AS

Tel: 01768 773030 · Fax: 01768 781099
publishing@mkupdate.co.uk
www.mkupdate.co.uk

Designed & typeset by Emphasis Communications

Foreword

This book is intended as a convenient guide for non-medical prescribers caring for patients with musculoskeletal problems. It includes an overview of the current legislation on prescribing and accountability and the principles of safe prescribing are clearly defined.

Chapters offer prescribing advice on disease-modifying drugs, biologics, pain control, systemic steroids and relevant medication for osteoporosis and gout. Basic information is provided on each drug, including the mechanism of action where known, evidence grading, dosage and contraindications. This book should therefore prove extremely relevant to autonomous practitioners requiring the evidence base and rationale to prescribe for patients with musculoskeletal disorders.

Naturally, although key side effects are listed, it was not possible to provide an exhaustive list for each drug in such a small volume. We suggest that practitioners check the British National Formulary (BNF – www.bnf.org/bnf/bnf/current, updated every six months) and the Summary of Product Characteristics (SPC – available at www.medicines.org.uk, updated daily) for new and all reported side effects, contraindications and interactions.

Julie Dawson
Sheena Hennell

Acknowledgements

The authors gratefully thank their reviewers – Ruth Sephton, Nicky Jeffries, Karen Herbert and Dawn Homer – for their helpful comments and support.

Chapter 1
Non-medical prescribing: the law and accountability

Chapter 2
Safe prescribing

Chapter 3
Analgesics

Chapter 4
Atypical analgesics

Chapter 5
Non-steroidal anti-inflammatory drugs (NSAIDs)

Chapter 6
Disease-modifying anti-rheumatic drugs (DMARDs)

Chapter 7
Biologic drugs

Chapter 8
Osteoporosis

Chapter 9
Allopurinol, colchicine and viscosupplementation

Chapter 10
Corticosteroids

References

List of figures

List of acronyms

BASDAI	Bath Ankylosing Spondylitis Disease Activity Index
BNF	British National Formulary
BSR	British Society for Rheumatology
CDs	controlled drugs
CMP	clinical management plan
CNS	central nervous system
CPD	continual professional development
CSM	Committee on the Safety of Medicines
DAS	disease activity score
DMARDs	disease-modifying anti-rheumatic drugs
EMEA	European Medicines Agency
FBC	full blood count
INR	international normalisation ratio
LFT	liver function test
MAOI	monoamine oxidase inhibitors
NICE	National Institute for Health and Clinical Excellence
NMC	Nursing and Midwifery Council
NSAIDs	non-steroidal anti-inflammatory drugs
NYHA	New York Heart Association
PsARC	Psoriatic Arthritis Response Criteria
RCP	Royal College of Physicians
s/c	subcutaneous
SERM	selective oestrogen receptor modulator
SLE	systemic lupus erythematosus
SPC	Summary of Product Characteristics
SSRIs	selective serotonin reuptake inhibitors
TCAs	tricyclic anti-depressants
U&E	urea and electrolytes
VAS	visual analogue scale
WHO	World Health Organisation

Non-Medical Prescribing: The law and accountability

1.1 Prescribing law

Nurses and pharmacists may prescribe from the full British National Formulary (BNF), with the exception of controlled drugs (CDs). However nurses in some specialist areas may prescribe from a small number of CDs for conditions indicated. Physiotherapists, chiropodists/podiatrists, radiographers and optometrists may supplementary prescribe. Pharmacists are currently not allowed to prescribe controlled drugs independently.

From 1 May 2006, the Nurse Prescribers' Extended Formulary was discontinued and qualified Nurse Independent Prescribers (formerly known as Extended Formulary Nurse Prescribers) are now entitled to prescribe any licensed medicine for any medical condition within their competence.

1.2 Guidance and standards

Guidance and standards exist and apply for all health professionals as detailed below.

The Nursing and Midwifery Council (NMC) has produced new standards of proficiency for nurse and midwife prescribers (NMC, 2006). The Department of Health (DH) has also produced guidance, published electronically on their website (DH, 2006).

Pharmacists must prescribe in accordance with *Medicines, Ethics and Practice* published by the Royal Pharmaceutical Society of Great Britain (RPSGB, 2006). Allied health professionals must act in accordance with the Health Professionals Council's *Standards of Conduct, Performance and Ethics* (HPC, 2004).

1.2 **Non-medical prescribing**

There are two methods of prescribing:

- independent prescribing
- supplementary prescribing.

Independent prescribing

The non-medical prescriber takes responsibility for the clinical assessment of the patient, establishing a diagnosis and the clinical management required as well as the responsibility for prescribing where necessary and the appropriateness of any prescription.

Nurse and Pharmacist Independent Prescribers

Nurse Independent Prescribing (formerly Extended Formulary Nurse Prescribing) was legalised in May 2006. Independent prescribing allows nurses who have completed the relevant training and with their employer's approval, to prescribe any licensed medicine for any medical condition that an individual nurse prescriber is competent to treat. This includes the palliative care use of the CDs diamorphine, morphine, diazepam, lorazepam, midazolam, or oxycodone.

Pharmacist Independent Prescribing was also introduced on 1 May 2006 and allows pharmacists who have completed the relevant training and with their employer's approval, to prescribe any licensed medicine for any medical condition that an individual pharmacist prescriber is competent to treat. This allows access to virtually the whole of the BNF with the exception of CDs and unlicensed medicines.

Supplementary prescribing

Supplementary prescribing is defined as a voluntary partnership between an independent prescriber (a doctor or dentist) and a supplementary prescriber, to implement an agreed patient-specific clinical management plan (CMP) with the patient's agreement.

Supplementary prescribing allows nurses, pharmacists and allied health professionals who have completed the relevant training and with their employer's approval to prescribe in a supplementary prescribing partnership.

Following assessment and diagnosis by the independent prescriber and agreement of the CMP, the supplementary prescriber may prescribe any medicine for the patient that is referred to in a patient-specific CMP. There is no formulary for supplementary prescribing and there are no restrictions on the medical conditions that can be managed under these arrangements.

Supplementary prescribing is also a useful mechanism to enable new independent nurse and pharmacist prescribers to develop their expertise and confidence in prescribing and where a team approach to prescribing is clearly appropriate.

Off-label/off-licence medicines

Nurse Independent Prescribers must take full responsibility for their pre-scribing, and should only prescribe 'off-label' where it is considered best practice to do so.

Unlicensed medicines

Nurse Independent Prescribers who are also supplementary prescribers can still prescribe unlicensed medicines as part of a supplementary pre-scribing arrangement, if the doctor agrees, using a CMP.

Be aware when prescribing that you are sure of the licensed indication, that you are confident that best practice allows for off-label prescribing or, if necessary, use supplementary prescribing as the catch-all.

1.3 Accountability

Accountability is the **professional** term for responsibility and is defined for non-medical prescribers in the NMC 'Standards of Proficiency for Nurse and Midwife Prescribers' (NMC, 2006). The NMC may take dis-ciplinary action when a nurse fails to follow guidelines for professional accountability.

Practice Standard 1

- You may only prescribe once you have successfully completed an NMC-approved programme and recorded this on the NMC register.

- You may only prescribe from the formulary linked to your recorded qualification and must comply with statutory requirements applicable to your prescribing practice.
- The ability to prescribe is a privilege granted to you by legislation and your employer and should be seen in this light.

Practice Standard 2

- You are professionally accountable for your prescribing decisions including actions and omissions and cannot delegate this accountability to any other person.
- You must only ever prescribe within your level of experience and competence acting in accordance with Clause 6 of the NMC Code of Professional Conduct: Standards for conduct, performance and ethics.
- If you move to another area of practice you must consider the requirements of your new role and only ever prescribe within your level of experience and competence.
- In order to prescribe for a patient or client you must satisfy yourself that you have undertaken a full assessment including a thorough history and where possible accessing a full clinical record.
- You are accountable for your decision to prescribe and must prescribe only where you have relevant knowledge of the patient's health and medical history
- You must ensure a risk assessment has been undertaken in respect of the patient's other current medication and any potential for confusion with other medicines.

(NMC, 2006)

1.4 Vicarious liability

Liability is the **legal** term for responsibility. If, for example, a practitioner breaches legislation setting out what they can do within their role this may be deemed a criminal act. Vicarious liability, where the employer takes legal responsibility for the actions of its staff, provides protection for non-medical prescribers (Caulfield, 2004). Those nurses prescribing in a self-employed capacity must consider personal insurance cover as vicarious liability is not applicable.

It is important to read and be aware of your employer's (NHS Trust's) prescribing policy. In some acute Trusts prescribing policies exclude nurses from prescribing cytotoxics. As such, if a nurse were to act outside the boundaries agreed with his or her employer, he or she would not be covered by vicarious liability and the employer's insurance policy would therefore not pay out. Professional indemnity cover as provided through RCN membership for example is vital for nurses in extended roles.

Safe prescribing

2.1 Principles of safe prescribing

The ability to prescribe safely and competently is a fundamental element of patient care. The following chapter gives an outline of the principles required to prescribe for patients safely.

Safe prescribing can be sub-divided as follows in order to minimise the chance of a medication or prescribing error:

- principles of therapeutics
- principles of treatment
- writing the prescription
- monitoring.

According to the National Coordinating Council for Medication Error Reporting and Prevention (2002) a prescribing error can be defined as 'a preventable action or omission that may contribute to inappropriate or harmful use of a medicine'.

2.2 Principles of therapeutics

Prior to prescribing it is important, during your consultation with and assessment of the patient, to be aware of the following.

- Have a good knowledge and understanding of the pharmacology. Weigh up both the potential benefits and the potential hazards of treatment and understand the reasons for variability in drug response.
- Base your prescribing choice on best evidence (Maxwell & Walley, 2002).
- Grade your evidence base. In this book we have used Royal College of Physicians (RCP) grading evidence which is found in the Clinical Effectiveness and Evaluation Unit's Concise Guide to Good Practice (available on the RCP website – www.rcplondon.ac.uk).

- Maintain continual professional development (CPD) by keeping up-to-date.
- Involve the patient in the prescribing decision. Patients who are informed and knowledgeable may be more compliant and this may improve concordance (Whiting *et al.*, 2002).

2.3 Principles of treatment

Prior to prescribing it is important to consider the following two checklists. Figure 2.1 will assist you with the prescribing decision and Figure 2.2 with the prescribing process once treatment has been chosen.

Figure 2.1 Prescribing decision checklist

Assessment and diagnosis.

Consider and discuss with the patient any alternatives to drug therapy.

If, following discussion, the patient wishes to take the drug:

    Choose appropriate drug, making an evidence-based decision.

    Check for any allergies.

    Check for any relative cautions. (Consider co-morbidity.)

    Check for any contraindications. (Is the patient pregnant or breast feeding?)

    Check for any drug interactions. (Consider concomitant medication.)

Figure 2.2 Prescribing process checklist

Choose appropriate route and dosage.

Discuss any potential side effects with the patient.

Make a plan to review and monitor the outcome.

Have a full and clear discussion with patient to aid concordance.

2.4 Writing the prescription

When writing the prescription, the following checklist may be useful.

- Ensure patient details are correct.
- Use generic drug names (not brand names) and avoid abbreviations.
- Ensure dose, frequency and route of administration are correct and appropriate. Avoid using the term 'as directed' and specify a minimum dose interval for 'as required' directions.
- Ensure the duration of the prescription is confirmed.
- Refer to the British National Formulary (BNF) and Summary of Product Characteristics (SPC).
- Consider your hospital or primary care prescribing policy and/or formulary.
- Consider National Institute for Clinical Excellence (NICE) and professional body guidance.
- Include your professional status, for example 'nurse independent prescriber', and signature.
- Ensure that your writing is easy to read.

2.5 Monitoring

When planning the monitoring and follow-up of a patient's progress following prescription, the following checklist may be useful.

- Advise the patient to report any reaction or side effect through the specialist nurse helpline or to their primary physician or pharmacist.
- Advise the patient to attend for monitoring if required and as per protocol.
- At follow-up appointments, review the indications for continuing to take the drug.
- Liaise and communicate with the patient's primary physician, hospital specialist and other relevant parties.

2.6 Compliance and concordance

The non-medical prescriber has an excellent opportunity to promote compliance with medication. Any consultation is a potential educational opportunity and an informed patient is much more likely to comply with medication.

A study by Barber *et al.* has shown that 30 per cent of patients with chronic diseases have missed at least one dose of medication from a new prescription by day 10, some intentionally (Barber *et al.*, 2004). Reasons included side effects, concerns and often a need for more information, particularly among those who intentionally chose not to comply.

Within supplementary prescribing, the clinical management plan (CMP) has encouraged concordance which literally means agreement and harmony. The non-medical prescriber actively encourages the patient to help with the decision-making process and establishes concordance through partnership agreement.

Concordance, however, requires active and effective communication and appropriate patient information and advice to succeed. It is particularly relevant if there is more than one treatment option available to patients, as in the case of biologic therapy when two or more interventions have equal chances of benefit. In this case, achieving concordance may well improve compliance with treatment, ensuring that patients are more able to voice concerns or discuss potential side effects with health professionals.

Analgesics

3.1 Overview

Assessing the patient and establishing the cause of their musculoskeletal pain is fundamental to prescribing appropriate medication. The definition of pain is an unpleasant feeling which may be associated with actual or potential tissue damage and which may have physical and emotional components. It is important to distinguish between pain and nociception. Nociception is a neurophysiological term and refers to specific activity in nerve pathways. Nociception is the transmission mechanism for physiological pain and does not incorporate psychological pain.

When considering all medication treatment options, it is useful to identify whether the patient's pain has one or more of four components:

- mechanical nociceptive
- inflammatory nociceptive
- neuropathic
- psychological.

In Chapter 4 we will discuss atypical analgesics for pain with a significant neuropathic or psychological component.

When prescribing for pain, use the World Health Organisation (WHO) pain management ladder. The analgesic ladder for nociceptive pain outlines a stepped change of analgesics starting with non-opioid, moving to weak opioid and then strong opioid (Figure 3.1). With non-opioid and weak opioid there is usually a ceiling dose. Once treated with strong opioid the dose can be titrated according to the patient's pain and no ceiling dosage is defined.

Figure 3.1 Analgesic ladder

Analgesic ladder	Group	Examples described in this chapter
Step 1	Non-opioid	Paracetamol
Step 2	Weak opioid	Codeine, tramadol
Step 3	Strong opioid	Morphine, oxycodone, fentanyl, buprenorphine

When prescribing analgesics for chronic pain always make sure that the patient has taken the analgesic on a regular (by the clock) basis prior to moving onto the next step of the analgesic ladder. Analgesics are more effective in preventing pain than in relieving established pain. If a patient is having daily pain but waits until the pain has become unbearable before taking a painkiller, they continue to be distressed for a further 20 to 30 minutes (longer for slow release preparations) as the tablet is being absorbed and transferred to the blood stream. The opportunity for an analgesic to work in that situation is greatly diminished and the emotional component of pain is increased. The patient may end up moving quickly up the analgesic ladder, suffering more side effects of medication, such as drowsiness and constipation, and then decide that the tablets have severe side effects that outweigh its benefits.

Medication overuse headaches

These can occur in patients with chronic use of analgesics. Headaches occur when analgesic levels trough, for example, a patient may wake up with a headache in morning. It is thought that pain-signalling mechanisms become more sensitive with constant suppression by pain-killing medication.

All analgesics can cause this problem and it is important to educate patients so that they are aware. This may then be sufficient to make them avoid taking further analgesics in an attempt to treat the medication overuse headache. However, with significant symptoms, analgesics may need to be gradually withdrawn to treat the headache.

3.2 Non-opioid (Step 1)

Paracetamol (Acetominophen)

This is first choice treatment for acute and chronic musculoskeletal pain. It is also effective at controlling a fever.

Mechanism of action

Currently thought to be through inhibiting prostaglandins in the brain resulting in raising the pain threshold.

Evidence grading

Grade A evidence for acute and chronic pain (osteoarthritis) (Barden *et al.*, 2004; Moore *et al.*, 1997; Zhang *et al.*, 2004).

Preparations

Tablets (500 mg), soluble tablets (500 mg), oral suspension (120 mg/5 ml, 250 mg/5ml), suppositories (250 mg, 500 mg).

Dosage

0.5–1.0 g every 4–6 hours (maximum dosage: 4 g (8 500 mg tablets)/day).

Side effects

Medication overuse headache.

Cautions

Liver disease and severe renal impairment.

Contraindications

Known hypersensitivity to paracetamol.

Interactions

* The speed of absorption of paracetamol may be increased by metoclopramide or domperidone.
* Reduced by colestyramine.
* Prolonged regular intake may increase the risk of bleeding for patients on warfarin or coumarins.

Check the BNF and SPC regularly for all reported side effects, contraindications and interactions.

Prescribing advice

Caution all patients against taking more than eight tablets a day. Serious liver damage can occur with only small increases above the normal limit (for example, 5 g a day) in susceptible individuals. It is not always possible to predict who is at high risk of susceptibility to liver damage.

Two groups of patients with high susceptibility are those that are at risk of cytochrome P450 induction (excess alcohol intake or medication (phenytoin, phenobarbitone, carbamazepine, rifampicin, St Johns Wort)) and those that have glutathione depletion (for example, from starvation, cystic fibrosis, HIV infection). Paracetamol should be tried on a regular 1 g (four times a day) regime prior to prescribing additional medication.

3.3 Weak opioid (Step 2)

Codeine

Most prescribing formularies will suggest codeine as the first line to try in this second step of the analgesic ladder. Weak opioids are often combined with paracetamol. If the paracetamol dose (see above) is limiting the dose of opioid in a combination tablet then consider prescribing the opioid and paracetamol separately.

Mechanism of action

Codeine is metabolised in the body by an enzyme process called demethylation to morphine. Only ten per cent of the compound is converted to morphine. This then stimulates the opioid (mu and kappa) receptors in the central nervous system to cause inhibition of the spinal and central processing of pain sensation.

Evidence grading

Grade A evidence for acute and chronic pain (de Craen *et al.*, 1996; Furlan *et al.*, 2006; Moore *et al.*, 1997)

Preparations

Tablets (15 mg, 30 mg, 60 mg), syrup (25 mg/5 ml). Codeine combined with paracetamol available as tablet, dispersible or effervescent, or capsules in the following strengths:

- co-codamol 8/500 = 8 mg codeine/500 mg paracetamol
- co-codamol 15/500 = 15 mg codeine/500 mg paracetamol
- co-codamol 30/500 = 30 mg codeine/500 mg paracetamol.

Dosage

30–60 mg every 4–6 hours (maximum: 240 mg/day).

Side effects

Commonly nausea, vomiting, constipation, dizziness, sweating, dependence, medication overuse headache.

Cautions

Use as low a dose as possible in elderly and patients with hypothyroidism, hypoadrenalism, chronic hepatic disease and renal insufficiency. As codeine may cause the release of histamine, it should be given with caution to asthmatics. Pregnancy and breast feeding.

Contraindications

Known hypersensitivity to any of the tablet constituents; respiratory depression; obstructive airways disease; paralytic ileus; head injury; raised intra-cranial pressure; acute alcoholism. As codeine may cause the release of histamine, it is advised that it should not be given during an asthma attack.

Interactions

- Other central nervous system depressants, including sedatives, phenothiazines, and alcohol, may result in respiratory depression or sedation.
- Monoamine oxidase inhibitors (MAOI), or within two weeks of MAOI therapy, enhanced sedative effect of codeine or anti-depressant effect of MAOI.
- Mexiletine – codeine delays absorption.
- Codeine antagonises effects of domperidone and metoclopramide on the gastro-intestinal activity.

Chapter 3

Check the BNF and SPC regularly for all reported side effects, contraindications and interactions.

Prescribing advice

The amount of codeine in combined preparations varies. It is important to be aware of the different dosages and combinations available and try and match them according to the control of pain and the side effects that the patients are prone to.

The conversion of codeine to morphine occurs in the liver and is catalysed by the cytochrome P450 enzyme CYP2D6. Approximately six to ten per cent of the Caucasian population have poorly functional CYP2D6 and codeine therefore fails to be effective as an analgesic in these patients but they still have its side effects (Eckhardt *et al.*, 1998). Dependence can occur after a short duration of treatment and withdrawal symptoms may develop on stopping the drug.

Tramadol

Use when codeine is ineffective or troublesome because of constipation. Tramadol may have less respiratory depression and may be less addictive than codeine.

Mechanism of action

Tramadol's analgesic properties are thought to be from the binding of sigma, kappa, mu opioid receptors, inhibition of noradrenaline reuptake, and serotonin release.

Evidence grading

Grade A evidence for acute, chronic and neuropathic pain (Furlan *et al.*, 2006; Hollingshead *et al.*, 2006).

Preparations

Capsules (50 mg), orodispersible tablets (50 mg) or soluble tablets (50 mg). Also:

- modified release tablets, twice daily regime (100 mg, 150 mg, 200 mg)
- modified release tablets, once daily regime (150 mg, 200 mg, 300 mg, 400 mg)
- modified release capsules, twice daily regime (50 mg, 100 mg, 150 mg, 200 mg).

Tramadol combined with paracetamol is 37.5 mg tramadol with 325 mg paracetamol tablets

Dosage

50–100 mg not more than 4-hourly. Modified release twice daily preparations: initially 50–100 mg twice daily. Once daily tablets: initially 100 mg daily. (Maximum dose: 400 mg/day.)

Side effects

Commonly nausea and vomiting (more common than with codeine), constipation, dizziness, sweating, dependence, medication overuse headache. Abdominal discomfort, hypotension, psychiatric disturbance (hallucinations) and convulsions can also occur.

Interactions

- Other central nervous system depressants, including sedatives, phenothiazines, and alcohol, may result in respiratory depression or sedation.

- Monoamine oxidase inhibitors (MAOI), or within two weeks of MAOI therapy, enhanced sedative effect of tramadol or anti-depressant effect of MAOI.

- May increase the potential for other seizure threshold-lowering drugs to cause convulsions, examples being selective serotonin re-uptake inhibitors (SSRIs), tricyclic anti-depressants (TCAs) and anti-psychotics.

- Isolated cases of serotonergic syndrome have been reported with the therapeutic use of tramadol in combination with other serotonergic agents such as selective serotonin re-uptake inhibitors (SSRIs).

- Carbamazepine results in markedly decreased serum concentrations of tramadol which may reduce analgesic effectiveness and shorten the duration of action.

- Warfarin and coumarin – may caused increased international normalisation ratio (INR) and bruising in some patients.

- The combination of mixed agonists/antagonists (for example, buprenorphine, nalbuphine, pentazocine) with tramadol is not recommended because it is theoretically possible that the analgesic effect of a pure agonist is reduced under these circumstances.

Chapter 3

Check the BNF and SPC regularly for all reported side effects, contraindications and interactions.

Contraindications

Known hypersensitivity to any of the tablet constituents; respiratory depression; obstructive airways disease; paralytic ileus; head injury; raised intra-cranial pressure; acute alcoholism; uncontrolled epilepsy, pregnancy and breast feeding. May also exacerbate asthma attacks.

Prescribing advice

For those patients taking 4- to 6-hourly regular doses of tramadol, consider changeover to the modified release preparations. If intolerant to tramadol then an alternative is Tramacet. This may have equal potency to tramadol by combining tramadol and paracetamol, but the lower tramadol dose results in an improved side effect profile. It has also been shown to be effective in controlling pain of fibromyalgia (Bennett *et al.*, 2003).

3.4 Strong opioids (Step 3)

The most commonly used strong opioids used for chronic musculoskeletal nociceptive pain in the UK – morphine, oxycodone, fentanyl, and buprenorphine – are considered below. The prescription of these drugs for musculoskeletal conditions must be by supplementary prescribing using a clinical management plan (CMP).

Morphine

Morphine should be used according to the Royal College of Physicians' guidance for chronic non-malignant pain (RCP, 2000). It is the first choice strong opioid in most hospital formularies for chronic non-malignant pain. However, many patients find it difficult to accept this medication because of the strong public perception that morphine is associated with cancer, addiction and death.

Mechanism of action

Morphine is thought to work through agonism of mu opioid receptor with a smaller contribution from agonism of the kappa opioid receptor.

Evidence grading

Grade A evidence for chronic pain (Furlan *et al.*, 2006).

Preparations

• Oral solution (10 mg/5ml, 30 mg/5ml and 100 mg/5ml)

- Tablets (10 mg, 20 mg, 50 mg)
- Suppositories (10 mg, 15 mg, 20 mg, 30 mg)
- Injection (10, 15, 20 and 30 mg/ml)
- Modified release oral preparations – see Dosage.

Dosage

No ceiling dose. (See Prescribing advice.) To be taken every 12 hours:

- tablets (5 mg, 10 mg, 15 mg, 30 mg, 60 mg, 100 mg, 200 mg)
- suspension (20 mg, 30 mg, 60 mg, 100 mg, 200 mg)
- capsules (10 mg, 30 mg, 60 mg, 100 mg, 200 mg).

To be taken every 24 hours: capsules (30 mg, 60 mg, 90 mg, 120 mg, 150 mg, 200 mg).

Side effects

The major risk of opioid excess is respiratory depression. This can be fatal. The most common side effects at usual doses are nausea, constipation, confusion, occasionally vomiting and medication overuse headaches. Physical and psychological dependence may appear after taking therapeutic doses for periods of just one to two weeks. Some cases of dependence have been observed after only two to three days. Withdrawal syndrome (nausea, vomiting, diarrhoea, anxiety and shivering) may occur a few hours after withdrawal of a prolonged treatment and is maximal between the 36th and 72nd hours.

Cautions

Use as low a dose as possible in the elderly and patients with hypothyroidism, hypoadrenalism, chronic hepatic disease, renal insufficiency, hypotension, epilepsy, asthma and prostatic hypertrophy.

Contraindications

Known hypersensitivity to any of the tablet constituents; respiratory depression; obstructive airways disease; paralytic ileus; head injury; raised intra-cranial pressure; acute alcoholic intoxication and delirium tremens; pregnancy and breast-feeding.

Check the BNF and SPC regularly for all reported side effects, contraindications and interactions.

Interactions

- Other central nervous system depressants, including sedatives, phenothiazines and alcohol, may result in respiratory depression or sedation.

- Monoamine oxidase inhibitors (MAOI), or within two weeks of MAOI therapy, enhanced sedative effect of opioid or anti-depressant effect of MAOI.

- Cyclizine may counteract the haemodynamic benefits of opioids.

- Opioid analgesics with some antagonist activity, such as buprenorphine, nalbuphine or pentazocine, may precipitate withdrawal symptoms in patients who have recently used pure agonists such as morphine.

- Mexiletine-concomitant opioid use delays its absorption.

- Antagonises effects of domperidone and metoclopramide on the gastro-intestinal activity.

Prescribing advice

Only prescribe opiates if you are aware of the Royal College of Physicians' prescribing advice (RCP, 2000) and this has been fully discussed with the patient. Remember that supplementary prescribing using a CMP in agreement with consultant or primary physician and patient, will also be required.

It must be emphasised that this is a guide to the dose of strong opioid required. Inter-patient variability requires that each patient is carefully titrated to the appropriate dose. Patients should be carefully monitored after any change in medication and titration of dose is to be expected. Patients and relatives need readily accessible support.

Start with 5–10 mg of morphine or 10–20 mg if full dosage step 2 analgesics have been used previously. Halve the dose in elderly or co-morbidity described above. Give a short acting (4-hourly) preparation and adjust the dose according to the pain. Once the pain is controlled, the patient's 24-hourly morphine requirement can be determined and this can then be given as two divided doses (12-hourly regime) or as a single, once daily, dose.

During the first week of morphine treatment troublesome nausea and vomiting is to be expected, so co-prescribe an anti-emetic as a routine. Domperidone (10 mg, three times a day), haloperidol (0.5 micrograms at night) and ondansetron (unlicensed indication) are most commonly

Chapter 3

used. Constipation is also so predictable that an adjuvant laxative should be prescribed.

Oxycodone

Oxycodone is a semi-synthetic pharmacologically-active full opioid agonist. It may cause more constipation than morphine but less nausea and hallucinations. It has a rapid onset of action.

Mechanism of action

It is a mu, kappa and delta opioid receptor agonist. It has no antagonist properties. It does not require conversion to oxymorphine to be effective.

Evidence grading

Grade A evidence for chronic non-malignant pain (Furlan *et al.*, 2006).

Preparations

- Capsules (5 mg, 10 mg, 20 mg)
- Liquid (5 mg/5 ml)
- Concentrate (10 mg/ml)
- Injection (10 mg/ml)
- Modified release tablets (5 mg, 10 mg, 20 mg, 40 mg, 80 mg) to be taken 12-hourly.

Dosage

No ceiling dose. For chronic non-malignant pain, 40 mg a day is the average dose to control symptoms.

Side effects

As with morphine, the major risk of opioid excess is respiratory depression. This can be fatal. The most common side effects at usual doses are nausea, constipation, confusion, occasionally vomiting and medication overuse headaches. Physical and psychological dependence may appear after taking therapeutic doses for periods of just one to two weeks. Some cases of dependence have been observed after only two to three days. Withdrawal syndrome (nausea, vomiting, diarrhoea, anxiety and shiver-

Check the BNF and SPC regularly for all reported side effects, contraindications and interactions.

ing) may occur a few hours after withdrawal of a prolonged treatment and is maximal between the 36th and 72nd hours.

Cautions

Adults with mild to moderate renal impairment and mild hepatic impairment. Halve the initial starting dose for opioid naive patients.

Contraindications

As for morphine, severe hepatic and renal impairment (creatinine clearance < 10 ml/min).

Interactions

- Other central nervous system depressants, including sedatives, phenothiazines and alcohol, may result in respiratory depression or sedation.
- Monoamine oxidase inhibitors (MAOI), or within two weeks of MAOI therapy, enhanced sedative effect of opioid or anti-depressant effect of MAOI.
- Inhibitors of cytochrome P450 quinidine, cimetidine, ketoconazole, erythromycin may inhibit metabolism of oxycodone.

Prescribing advice

The usual starting dose for opioid naive patients or patients presenting with severe pain uncontrolled by weaker opioids, is 5 mg, 4- to 6-hourly. The dose should then be carefully titrated, as frequently as once a day if necessary, to achieve pain relief.

Patients receiving oral morphine before oxycodone therapy should have their daily dose based on the following ratio: 10 mg of oral oxycodone is equivalent to 20 mg of oral morphine. This again will require supplementary prescribing.

Fentanyl

Eighty times more potent than morphine and can only be used in opioid tolerant patients. It is probably less constipating than morphine. Only fentanyl, as patches, is licensed for chronic non-malignant pain.

Mechanism of action

A synthetic opioid with high affinity for the mu-opioid receptor.

Evidence grading

Grade A evidence for chronic pain from osteoarthritis (Langford *et al.*, 2006).

Preparations

Patches: '12' (releasing approx. 12 micrograms/hour for 72 hours), '25' (releasing approx. 25 micrograms/hour for 72 hours), '50' (releasing approx. 50 micrograms/hour for 72 hours), '75' (releasing approx. 75 micrograms/hour for 72 hours), '100' (releasing approx. 100 micrograms/hour for 72 hours).

Dosage

Start at '25' patch in patients who are strong opioid naive. In those already receiving strong opioid, then 90 mg of oral morphine over 24 hours is approximately equivalent to a 25 micrograms an hour fentanyl patch. A conversion table is available on electronic medicines compendium website (www.medicines.org.uk). As the serum levels gradually increase after applying the patch, allow at least 24 hours of treatment before changing dose.

At 300 micrograms/hour alternative treatment for pain should be considered.

Side effects

The most serious adverse reaction is respiratory suppression. Other opioid-related adverse reactions include: nausea; vomiting; constipation; hypotension; bradycardia; somnolence; headache; confusion; hallucinations; euphoria; pruritus; sweating and urinary retention. Involuntary muscle contractions may occur. Occasionally, skin reactions such as rash, erythema and itching have been reported. Reactions will usually resolve within 24 hours of patch removal. Opioid withdrawal symptoms are possible in some patients following conversion from their previous analgesic to fentanyl patches.

Cautions

Bradyarrhythmias, chronic respiratory disease, raised intra-cranial pressure, significant liver disease, and fever.

Check the BNF and SPC regularly for all reported side effects, contraindications and interactions.

Contraindications

As for morphine: known hypersensitivity to any of the patch constituents; respiratory depression; obstructive airways disease; paralytic ileus; head injury; raised intra-cranial pressure; acute alcoholic intoxication and delirium tremens; pregnancy and breast-feeding.

Interactions

* Other central nervous system depressants, including sedatives, phenothiazines and alcohol, may result in respiratory depression or sedation.

* Monoamine oxidase inhibitors (MAOI), or within two weeks of MAOI therapy, enhanced sedative effect of opioid or anti-depressant effect of MAOI.

* Ritonavir may result in an increase in fentanyl plasma concentrations.

Prescribing advice

The patient should have had full dosage of weak opioid before transfer to patch. (See morphine prescribing advice.) Titrate the dose up by adding fentanyl '12' patch. Routinely prescribe an anti-emetic for first week of treatment.

The patch should be applied to clean, dry, non-irritated, non-hairy flat area of upper arm or body. The transdermal patch should be pressed firmly in place for approximately 30 seconds, making sure the contact is complete, especially around the edges. On changing to a new patch this should then be applied to a different skin site. Advise the patient to wait several days before a new patch is applied to the same area of skin.

Heat (whether internal (for example, fever) or external (for example, a sauna)) can potentially increase fentanyl delivery rate. It is necessary to avoid exposure to external heat, or monitor for opioid side effects if there is a significant increase in body temperature.

It may take 22 hours or longer for plasma fentanyl levels to decrease by 50 per cent when a patch is removed and not replaced. Alternative opioid treatment should be initiated at a low dose and titrated slowly.

Buprenorphine

This drug is a mixed agonist/antagonist used for moderate to severe pain. It is not administered orally, due to very high first pass metabolism. Opiate antagonist effects are not usually seen when combined with weak opioid, however it can precipitate withdrawal symptoms in patients physically dependent on full agonist opiates. Its effects can only be partially blocked by naloxone.

Mechanism of action

Synthetic opioid, partially stimulates the mu opioid receptors, kappa opioid receptor antagonist.

Evidence grading

Grade A evidence for chronic pain (Sorge & Sittl, 2004).

Preparation

- Once-weekly transdermal patches: '5' (releasing 5 micrograms/hour for 7 days), '10' (releasing 10 micrograms/hour for 7 days), '20' (releasing 20 micrograms/hour for 7 days).
- Twice-weekly transdermal patches: '35' (releasing 35 micrograms/ hour for 96 hours), '52.5' (releasing 52.5 micrograms/hour for 96 hours), '70' (releasing 70 micrograms/hour for 96 hours).
- Sublingual tablets (200 and 400microgram).

Dosage

- Patches. (See Prescribing advice.)
- Sublingual tablets (200–400 micrograms 8-hourly).

Side effects

Similar to those of other opioids and include nausea and vomiting, drowsiness, dizziness, headache, itchiness, dry mouth, miosis, orthostatic hypotension, male ejaculatory difficulty, decreased libido, urinary retention, constipation, physical and psychological dependence. Local reactions to the patches are common.

Cautions

Convulsive disorders, head injury, reduced level of consciousness of uncertain origin, intra-cranial lesions or increased intra-cranial pressure. Patients with severe hepatic impairment.

Check the BNF and SPC regularly for all reported side effects, contraindications and interactions.

Contraindications

Hypersensitivity to any of the excipients; conditions in which the respiratory centre and function are severely impaired or may become so; patients suffering from myasthenia gravis or delirium tremens. Pregnancy and breast feeding.

Interactions

- Monoamine oxidase inhibitors (MAOI), or within two weeks of MAOI therapy, enhanced sedative effect of opioid or anti-depressant effect of MAOI.

- Strong opioid – may precipitate withdrawal symptoms.

Prescribing advice

Remember that supplementary prescribing, using a clinical management plan (CMP) and agreement with consultant or primary physician and patient, will be required. Patients do not need to be on full dosage of mild opioid to convert to buprenorphine patches. Where the patient is going to require district nurses or family members to apply the patch, the seven-day preparation has an obvious advantage over the 96-hour patches. The fact that the narcotic effects of overdose cannot be reversed by naloxone, is of major concern, and buprenorphine should be avoided in patients thought to be at risk of overdosing (either deliberately or inadvertently).

The patch should be applied to a clean, dry, non-irritated, non-hairy flat area of upper arm or body. The transdermal patch should be pressed firmly in place for approximately 30 seconds, making sure the contact is complete, especially around the edges. A new patch should be applied to a different skin site. Advise the patient to wait several days before a new patch is applied to the same area of skin.

Heat internal (for example, fever) or external (for example, a sauna) can potentially increase buprenorphine delivery rate. It is necessary to avoid exposure to external heat, or monitor for opioid side effects if there is a significant increase in body temperature.

It may take 10 to 24 hours or longer for plasma buprenorphine levels to decrease by 50 per cent when a patch is removed and not replaced. Alternative opioid treatment should be avoided for 24 hours after removing the patch if possible.

Atypical analgesics

4.1 Overview

These are medications that are effective for pain but are not utilising the opioid receptor pathway. They are usually for neuropathic pain or have been demonstrated to be of help in chronic pain syndromes such as fibromyalgia. These medicines were originally introduced for the treatment of depression or epilepsy. Now they are being designed specifically to treat neuropathic pain.

Symptoms of neuropathic pain are spontaneous pain which is frequently described as shooting, burning or electric shock-like. Frequently it can be indescribable. Often it is associated with the symptoms of numbness and pins and needles. Signs are hyperalgesia (increased sensation of pain in response to normally painful stimuli) and allodynia (pain in response to normally non-painful stimuli).

Capsaicin is a topical treatment for neuropathic pain and also has been shown to be mildly effective in controlling the pain of osteoarthritis. Tramadol and oxycodone (described in Chapter 3) have also been shown to be effective for neuropathic pain.

4.2 Amitriptyline and nortriptyline

Although widely used for neuropathic pain, and where there is significant sleep disturbance associated with chronic pain, these drugs are not actually licensed for pain. They are licensed as anti-depressants and for nocturnal enuresis. Nortriptyline is the principle active metabolite of amitriptyline.

Mechanism of action

The precise mechanism of action is unknown. They have anti-cholinergic and sedative properties and prevent the re-uptake of noradrenaline and serotonin at nerve terminals.

Evidence grading

Grade A evidence for chronic pain, chronic neuropathic pain and chronic low back pain (McQuay *et al.*, 1992; Pheasant *et al.*, 1983; Saarto & Wiffen, 2005).

Preparations

- Amitriptyline tablets (10 mg, 25 mg, 50 mg)
- Amitriptyline oral solution (25 mg/5 ml, 50 mg/5 ml)
- Nortriptyline tablets (10 mg, 25 mg).

Dosage

Usually 10 mg–75 mg nocte. Use the lowest possible dose in elderly people and adolescents.

Side effects

Drowsiness, dizziness, postural hypotension, nausea, constipation, blurred vision, dry mouth, difficulty with micturition, elevation of blood sugar level. Lower seizure threshold.

Cautions

Epilepsy, closed angle glaucoma, liver disease, cardiac disease particularly with arrhythmias, thyrotoxicosis, psychoses, prostatic hypertrophy or urinary retention, porphyria.

Contraindications

Hypersensitivity to amitriptyline or nortriptyline, recent myocardial infarction, pregnancy and breast feeding.

Interactions

- Monoamine oxidase inhibitors (MAOI), or within two weeks of MAOI therapy, enhanced sedative effect of opioid or anti-depressant effect of MAOI.
- Sympathomimetic drugs – adrenaline/epinephrine, ephedrine, isoprenaline.
- Noradrenaline/norepinephrine, phenylephrine and phenylpropanolamine.
- Decrease the anti-hypertensive effect of guanethidine, bethanidine and possibly clonidine.
- Barbiturates may increase their rate of metabolism.

- Anaesthetics given during tricyclic anti-depressant therapy may increase the risk of arrhythmias and hypotension.

- Other central nervous system depressants, including sedatives, phenothiazines and alcohol, may result in sedation.

- Higher than expected steady-state serum concentrations of the tricyclic anti-depressant have been observed when therapy is initiated in patients already taking cimetidine. A decrease may occur when cimetidine therapy is discontinued.

- Any drug that utilises the hepatic cytochrome P450IID6 isoenzyme system, may compete for metabolism by this system and lead to drug interactions. Lower doses than are usually prescribed for either the tricyclic anti-depressant or the other drug may therefore be required. Examples of drugs that are metabolised by this isoenzyme, including other anti-depressants: fluoxetine, phenothiazines, carbamazepine, propafenone, flecainide.

- Drugs that inhibit this enzyme (for example, quinidine) should be approached with caution.

- Other anti-cholinergic drugs.

- Tricyclic anti-depressants can lower seizure threshold and may antagonise the effect of anti-epileptic drugs.

Prescribing advice

Spend at least five minutes explaining to the patient how to take the tablets, potential side effects and that they are anti-depressants (albeit that they are being used at a much lower dose and as a treatment for pain). This, in our experience, does improve compliance and avoids needless prescriptions. Remember that amitriptyline or nortriptyline are prescribed 'off-label' (unlicensed indication) in this instance.

In patients who are not taking any other drugs acting on the central nervous system (CNS), who are of normal body weight and not particularly prone to side effects, start with 25 mg amitriptyline and increase by 25 mg increments every two to three weeks. The effective dose can be anywhere between 10 and 75 mg per day. If it works at a low dose and the patient benefits, they may remain on that dose.

Chapter 4

Check the BNF and SPC regularly for all reported side effects, contraindications and interactions.

In susceptible or particularly cautious patients, start at 10 mg of amitriptyline and, if side effects occur with this, switch to 10 mg of nortriptyline.

Amitriptyline can be taken two to four hours before planned sleep, rather than at bedtime. This helps to reduce hangover effect in the morning. Warn the patients about this and also warn them about dizziness and tiredness. Encourage them to keep taking the tablets despite this as, with time, it is likely to settle. Discourage the use of alcohol while taking these tablets. Drivers and operators of heavy machinery should be advised to be cautious of this side effect, as if the 'hangover' effect is significant they will need to avoid these activities until it settles. It may be best to start the tablets at the weekend.

Advise the patient that these tablets need to be taken regularly to be most effective. Sleep improvement may occur quite quickly but improved pain control can take two to three weeks. Recommend that if patients find amitriptyline helpful they should continue it for a minimum of six months. Withdrawal symptoms can occur on suddenly stopping amitriptyline or nortriptyline (nausea, headache, dizziness). Whilst these drugs are not addictive it is suggested that, in order to minimise withdrawal symptoms, patients should be gradually weaned off them rather than stopped abruptly.

4.3 Gabapentin

Licensed for neuropathic pain.

Mechanism of action

Similar in structure to the neurotransmitter GABA but is not believed to act on the same brain receptors. Its exact mechanism of action is unknown, but its therapeutic action on neuropathic pain is thought to be due to binding to the alpha 2-delta subunit of the voltage-dependent calcium ion channel in the central nervous system, blocking channel action and thus calcium influx.

Evidence grading

Grade A evidence for chronic neuropathic pain (Wiffen *et al.*, 2005).

Preparations

- Capsules (100 mg, 300 mg, 400 mg)
- Tablets (600 mg, 800 mg).

Chapter 4

Dosage

300 mg–1800 mg a day. Dose titration is required.

Side effects

Gabapentin has an extensive list of common side effects, as such we suggest looking up any reported side effect on product information (SPC). Most common however are nausea, dry mouth, arthralgia, dizziness, drowsiness, constipation, loss of appetite, skin itching, sore gums, indigestion, sexual difficulties, restlessness, weight gain, tremor, slurred speech, or pain/burning/tingling in the hands/feet, oedema, diarrhoea, flatulence, leucopenia and diplopia.

Cautions

Elderly and renal impairment – reduce dose.

Contraindications

Hypersensitivity to gabapentin. Pregnancy and breast feeding.

Interactions

- Antacids can reduce absorption so avoid taking for two hours after antacid.

- Other central nervous system depressants, including sedatives, phenothiazines and alcohol, may result in sedation.

Prescribing advice

Gabapentin can be very effective for neuropathic pain, however, in general, tricyclic anti-depressants are tolerated better. So use gabapentin when patients have neuropathic pain and are intolerant to tricyclic anti-depressants or when they are ineffective, contraindicated or the patient refuses to take anti-depressants (after a reasoned discussion).

In relatively healthy adults, the Neurontin (branded gabapentin) titration pack (to 1800 mg) is well tolerated. This pack is under patent and is relatively expensive. However, once the patient is established on 600 mg three times a day of gabapentin it can be prescribed generically.

Chapter 4

Check the BNF and SPC regularly for all reported side effects, contraindications and interactions.

In the elderly and those with significant co-morbidity, prescribe 300 mg a day and increase weekly by 300 mg, aiming for 300 mg three times a day. Some patients may respond to a lower dose.

Warn the patient about dizziness and somnolence and explain that, if they can tolerate them, they should settle after the dose has been stable for three weeks. The tablets need to be taken regularly and can take four to six weeks to have full effect.

Drivers and operators of heavy machinery should be advised to be cautious of the somnolence side effect and, if it is significant, they will need to avoid these activities until it settles. It may be best to start the tablets at the weekend.

If treatment is ineffective or the patient has surgical decompression of the nerve and no longer needs gabapentin, it is advised to withdraw treatment slowly (because sudden withdrawal can cause anxiety, insomnia, nausea, pain and sweating). We suggest reducing the dose by 300 mg every three days.

4.4 Pregabalin

Licensed for neuropathic pain. Pregabalin is excellent for neuropathic pain. It does not require the lengthy titration of gabapentin, is tolerated well and benefits can be seen at one week.

Mechanism of action

Like gabapentin, pregabalin binds to the alpha2-delta subunit of the voltage-dependent calcium ion channel in the central nervous system, blocking channel action and thus calcium influx. However, the exact mechanism of action is unknown.

Evidence grading

Grade A evidence for chronic neuropathic pain, however trials are 12 weeks' duration or less (Freynhagen et al., 2005).

Preparations

Capsules (25 mg, 50 mg, 75 mg, 100 mg, 150 mg, 200 mg, 225 mg, 300 mg).

Dosage

75 mg–300 mg twice daily.

Side effects

Dizziness, drowsiness, visual disturbance, ataxia, dysarthria, euphoria, oedema, tremor, lethargy, memory impairment, weight gain, constipation, dry mouth.

Cautions

Renal impairment – dose needs to be reduced. Elderly patients – prone to falls with dizziness.

Contraindications

Hypersensitivity to pregabalin. Pregnancy and breast feeding.

Interactions

Other central nervous system depressants, including sedatives, phenothiazines and alcohol, may result in sedation.

Prescribing advice

Use the twice a day dosage (which is cheaper than three times a day dosage and effective in the pain trials) and start at 75 mg daily and increase after a week to 75 mg twice a day. This dose is usually effective but if needed it can be increased to 300 mg twice a day. The main side effect is somnolence. Warn the patient of this and see whether they can tolerate it initially as it may settle after a few weeks. In sensitive patients 25 mg dosage can be used. As opposed to amitriptyline, pregabalin is licenced for neuropathic pain but has the additional benefits of improved sleep, improved depression scores and an anxiolytic effect. It is advised to withdraw treatment slowly because sudden withdrawal can cause anxiety, insomnia, nausea, pain and sweating. Stop treatment gradually over one week.

Check the BNF and SPC regularly for all reported side effects, contraindications and interactions.

4.5 Duloxetine hydrochloride

Duloxetine hydrochloride or Cymbalta is licensed to treat pain related to diabetic peripheral neuropathy.

Mechanism of action

Duloxetine is a re-uptake inhibitor of serotonin and noradrenaline, which lacks affinity for monoamine receptors within the central nervous system.

Evidence grading

Grade A evidence for diabetic peripheral neuropathy (Raskin *et al.*, 2005).

Preparation

Capsules (30 mg, 60 mg).

Dosage

60 mg daily.

Side effects

Most commonly (greater than ten per cent of patients) headache, somnolence, nausea, dry mouth, diarrhoea, anxiety, decreased libido, agitation, abnormal dreams, dizziness, tremor, nervousness, paraesthesia, blurred vision, palpitations, yawning, constipation, vomiting, dyspepsia, flatulence, increased sweating, rash, musculoskeletal pain, muscle tightness, erectile dysfunction, fatigue, abdominal pain, decreased appetite.

Withdrawal symptoms when treatment is discontinued are common. They include dizziness, sensory disturbances, sleep disturbances, agitation or anxiety, nausea and vomiting, tremor, and headache.

Cautions

A history of mania or seizures, increased intra-ocular pressure or those at risk of acute narrow-angle glaucoma, pre-existing hypertension. Medical conditions which could be compromised by tachycardia or hypertension. Those at increased risk for hyponatraemia, for example the elderly, patients with cirrhosis or dehydration, or patients treated with diuretics.

Contraindications

Hypersensitivity or intolerance to the active substance or to any of the excipients, liver disease resulting in hepatic impairment, severe renal impairment (creatinine clearance < 30 ml/min), uncontrolled hypertension. Pregnancy and breast feeding.

Interactions

- Other central nervous system depressants, including sedatives, phenothiazines and alcohol, may result in sedation.
- Monoamine oxidase inhibitors (MAOI), or within two weeks of MAOI therapy, enhanced sedative effect of opioid or anti-depressant effect of MAOI.
- SSRIs, tricyclics anti-depressants, St John's Wort, venlafaxine, or triptans, tramadol, pethidine and tryptophan may increase risk of serotonin syndrome development.
- Drugs that are predominantly metabolised by CYP2D6 (risperidone, tricyclic anti-depressants) particularly if they have a narrow therapeutic index (such as flecainide, propafenone and metoprolol).
- Anticoagulants and anti-platelet agents – potential increased risk of bleeding and increases in INR values have been reported when duloxetine has been co-prescribed with warfarin.
- Potent inhibitors of CYP1A2 like fluvoxamine inhibit metabolism of duloxetine and should not be used together.
- Inducers of CYP1A2: smokers have almost 50 per cent lower plasma concentrations of duloxetine compared with non-smokers.

Prescribing advice

Due to an unattractive side effect profile, duloxetine tends to be used when the other atypical analgesics have failed or not been tolerated. Currently no comparison with existing treatments has been published. Duloxetine is also being used to treat pain symptoms in patients with fibromyalgia at a dose of 60 mg twice daily (Arnold *et al.*, 2005). This is 'off-label' (unlicensed indication) prescribing.

In patients with fibromyalgia who are sensitive to the side effects of medication, we suggest starting at 30 mg once a day, increasing on a fortnightly basis to 60 mg twice a day or highest tolerated dose.

Check the BNF and SPC regularly for all reported side effects, contraindications and interactions.

Because of the withdrawal side effects of duloxetine it is advised that duloxetine should be gradually tapered when discontinuing treatment over a period of not less than two weeks, according to the patient's needs.

Monitoring

In patients with known hypertension or other cardiac disease, blood pressure monitoring is recommended, especially during the first month of treatment.

4.6 Capsaicin

Derived from chilli pepper plants and licensed for use in osteoarthritis and peripheral neuropathy, it is only mildly effective but may be suitable for patients who cannot tolerate or respond to other treatments.

Mechanism of action

The chemical compound capsaicin (8-methyl-N-vanillyl-6-nonenamide), if used regularly, results in the neurotransmitter, substance P being depleted from neurones.

Evidence grading

Grade A evidence (Mason *et al.*, 2004a).

Preparation

Topical cream (0.025 per cent, 0.075 per cent).

Dosage

- Osteoarthritis – 0.025 per cent cream four times daily.
- Painful diabetic peripheral neuropathy and herpes zoster neuralgic pain – 0.075 per cent cream four times daily (for 8 weeks then review).

Side effects

Initial burning sensations may be distressing but reduce after the first few applications.

Cautions

Avoid contact with eyes, inflamed or delicate skin. Not to be used under tight bandages. Allergy to chillies.

Contraindications

Hypersensitivity to any of the constituents.

Prescribing advice

Tell the patient to apply only a pea size amount of cream to the affected area four times daily and not more often than every four hours. The cream should be rubbed in until there is no residue left on the skin surface. The applying finger should be washed immediately after application of the cream.

Advise the patient that the analgesic effect usually begins within the first week of treatment and increases with continuing regular application for the next two to eight weeks. Patients should avoid taking a shower or hot bath just before or after applying capsaicin, as it can increase the burning sensation.

For use of the 0.075 per cent cream, hospital consultant supervision is currently recommended.

Check the BNF and SPC regularly for all reported side effects, contraindications and interactions.

Non-steroidal anti-inflammatory drugs (NSAIDs)

5.1 Traditional and Cox-2 NSAIDs

NSAIDs are licensed for mild to moderate pain and inflammation in rheumatic disease and other musculoskeletal disorders. They have analgesic, anti-pyretic and anti-inflammatory effect and can be combined with other painkillers. This chapter will cover traditional NSAIDs (specifically ibuprofen, naproxen and diclofenac), Cox-2 NSAIDs (specifically celecoxib and etoricoxib) and topical NSAIDs.

Mechanism of action

NSAIDs work by cyclo-oxygenase inhibition of the prostaglandin pain pathway in the peripheral nervous system. With cyclo-oxygenase isoenzyme 2 inhibitors, they preferentially inhibit prostaglandins involved in pain and inflammation above cyclo-oxygenase 1 inhibitors that are involved in constitutional functions, such as gastroprotection.

Evidence grading

Grade A evidence in acute back pain, rheumatoid arthritis, osteoarthritis, gout, ankylosing spondylitis (Collantes *et al.*, 2002; Schumacher Jr. *et al.*, 2002; van Tulder *et al.*, 2000; Zhang *et al.*, 2004; Zochling *et al.*, 2006).

Preparations

See Dosage.

Dosage – Non-selective NSAIDs

Ibuprofen: 1.2–1.8 g/day in 3–4 divided doses (maximum dose 2.4 g/day). Available as tablets (200 mg, 400 mg, 600 mg), oral suspension, syrup, granules and as modified release tablets (800 mg) or capsules (300 mg). Available over the counter.

Naproxen: (for acute pain) 500 mg initially (750 mg in gout) followed by 250 mg every 6–8 hours; (for chronic rheumatic disease) 250 mg–500 mg twice a day. Available as tablets (250 mg, 375 mg, 500 mg).

Diclofenac: 150 mg/day in 2–3 divided doses. Available as tablets (25 mg, 50 mg), modified release capsules and tablets (75 mg and 100 mg) and suppositories (12.5 mg, 25 mg, 50 mg, 100 mg).

Dosage – Cox-2 selective NSAIDs

Celecoxib: (for osteoarthritis and elderly) 200 mg/day in 1–2 divided doses; (for rheumatoid arthritis) 200–400 mg/day in 2 divided doses. Available as capsules (100 mg and 200 mg).

Etoricoxib: (for acute gout) 120 mg, as 7-day pack of tablets; (for osteoarthritis) 60 mg/day tablets; (for rheumatoid arthritis) 90 mg/day tablets.

Side effects

Nausea, vomiting, dyspepsia, abdominal pain, flatulence, diarrhoea, vomiting blood, malaena, peptic ulcers, perforation, fluid retention, hypertension, aggravated asthma, rashes including photosensitivity. Nephrotoxicity in various forms, including interstitial nephritis, nephrotic syndrome and renal failure. Also abnormal liver function, hepatitis and jaundice. Visual disturbances, optic neuritis, headaches, paraesthesia, reports of aseptic meningitis, confusion, hallucinations, tinnitus, vertigo, dizziness, malaise, fatigue and drowsiness.

Cautions

- In elderly and patients with cardiovascular, renal and hepatic impairment, NSAIDs cause a dose-dependent reduction in prostaglandin formation and can precipitate renal failure. Renal function should be monitored in these patients.
- Patients with a history of heart failure and hypertension since fluid retention and oedema has been reported in association with use of NSAIDs.
- Cyclooxygenase 2 specific inhibitors and patients with risk factors for developing heart disease.
- Patients with asthma, since NSAIDs have been reported to cause bronchospasm.
- A history of gastro-intestinal disease (ulcerative colitis, Crohn's Disease) as these conditions may be exacerbated.
- Patients with systemic lupus erythematosus (SLE) and mixed connective tissue disorders. There may be an increased risk of aseptic meningitis.

Chapter 5

- In women attempting to conceive, the use of NSAIDs may impair female fertility and is not recommended. In women who have difficulties conceiving or who are undergoing investigation of infertility, withdrawal of NSAIDs should be considered.

Contraindications

In patients with a known sensitivity to any of its constituents or in response to ibuprofen, aspirin or other non-steroidal anti-inflammatory drugs. Patients with a history of, or active, peptic ulcer, history of, or active, upper gastro-intestinal bleeding or perforation related to previous NSAID therapy. Severe liver, renal or cardiac failure. During the last trimester of pregnancy. Combined with other NSAIDs including the cyclooxygenase 2 specific inhibitors.

Etoricoxib is contraindicated in patients with hypertension whose blood pressure is not under control.

Cyclooxygenase 2-specific inhibitors are contraindicated in ischaemic heart disease, cerebrovascular disease, peripheral vascular disease and moderate or severe heart failure.

Interactions

- Lithium: may increase plasma concentrations and decrease elimination of lithium.
- Cardiac glycosides: increase plasma glycoside levels.
- Anti-coagulants: may enhance the effects of anti-coagulants, such as warfarin.
- Antidiabetic agents: isolated reports of hyperglycaemic and hypoglycaemic effects, which have required adjustments to the dosage of hypoglycaemic agents.
- Ciclosporin: nephrotoxicity may be increased by the effect of NSAIDs on renal prostaglandins.
- Mifepristone: NSAIDs should not be used for 8–12 days after mifepristone administration as NSAIDs can reduce its effect.
- Quinolone antibiotics: patients taking NSAIDs and quinolones may have an increased risk of developing convulsions.
- Therapy with aspirin may increase the frequency of side effects.

Check the BNF and SPC regularly for all reported side effects, contraindications and interactions.

- Corticosteroids: NSAIDs can increase the risk of gastro-intestinal bleeding.

- Diuretics: NSAIDs inhibit the activity of diuretics. Diuretics can increase the risk of nephrotoxicity of NSAIDs. Concomitant treatment with potassium-sparing diuretics may be associated with increased serum potassium levels. Serum potassium should be monitored.

- Anti-hypertensives: reduced anti-hypertensive effect.

- Tacrolimus: possible increased risk of nephrotoxicity when NSAIDs are given with tacrolimus.

Prescribing advice

When prescribing an NSAID, consider the risks of serious gastro-intestinal complication and cardiovascular disease. The prescribing of NSAIDs and associated cardiovascular risk has been highly publicised and new guidance is produced at regular intervals. The British National Formulary has the latest Committee on Safety of Medicines (CSM) advice. Also be aware of National Institute for Health and Clinical Excellence (NICE) and European Medicines Agency (EMEA) guidance on NSAIDs.

The most recent advice has been that all NSAIDs (non-selective or selective Cox-2 inhibitors) can increase blood pressure by 3–5 mmHg, an amount that explains the increase in stroke, angina and heart failure seen in recent studies (Madhok *et al.*, 2006). We suggest that you try and avoid all NSAIDs in patients who have ischaemic heart or cerebrovascular disease.

The high risk group for gastro-intestinal complications are those: aged over 65, concomitantly using medications likely to increase gastro-intestinal side effects – such as anti-coagulants, corticosteroids; with serious co-morbidity; requiring prolonged use of maximum recommended doses of standard NSAIDs; and with a previous history of peptic ulcer with or without complications. In these patients, if an NSAID is justified then gastroprotection (usually proton pump inhibitor) and traditional NSAID or a Cox-2 NSAID will be required.

Try and use the lowest effective dose of NSAID for the shortest possible duration of treatment. Most are taken with food.

NSAIDs have a highly variable effect between patients so it is always worth trying two or three to find one that suits that individual, but allow up to four weeks of taking the NSAID on a regular basis for full anti-inflammatory effect. For gout, treatment of the acute attack, use NSAIDs at their highest licensed dose and tailor down the dose as the signs of inflammation settle. Those NSAIDs that have been shown to be effective in gout are indometacin, piroxicam and etoricoxib (Cobra *et al.*, 1983; Schumacher Jr *et al.*, 2002).

5.2 Topical NSAIDs

Effective in the treatment of osteoarthritis of superficial joints such as the knee, acute musculoskeletal injuries, periarthritis, epicondylitis, tendinitis, and tenosynovitis.

Mechanism of action

Inhibits prostaglandin synthesis and release through inhibition of the cyclo-oxygenase enzyme.

Evidence grading

Grade A evidence for one-week treatment of acutely painful conditions (Mason *et al.*, 2004b).

Preparations

Gels, cutaneous solution, foam, and gel patch. Available over the counter.

Dosage

Apply to the area affected, two to four times daily, except patch (apply one patch for 72 hours).

Side effects

Mild to moderate local irritation, erythema, pruritus and dermatitis and photosensitive skin reaction. Minor gastro-intestinal side effects such as nausea, dyspepsia, abdominal pain and dyspnoea.

Cautions

Patients with impaired liver or renal function.

> Check the BNF and SPC regularly for all reported side effects, contraindications and interactions.

Contraindications

Hypersensitivity to constituents or in response to ibuprofen, aspirin or other non-steroidal anti-inflammatory drugs.

Prescribing advice

Avoid eyes and mucosal surfaces. Do not apply to any sites affected by open skin lesions, skin diseases or infection. To avoid possibility of photosensitivity advise patients against excessive exposure of treated area to sunlight. Effectiveness only demonstrated in short-term use. Review prescription after two to four weeks.

Disease-modifying anti-rheumatic drugs (DMARDs)

6.1 Overview

Disease-modifying anti-rheumatic drugs (DMARDs) can suppress the disease process and reduce the progression of disease. Be aware that this is a specialist area. Only prescribe if you are familiar with the British Society for Rheumatology DMARD guidance (BSR, 2007).

Under specialist supervision and using agreed protocols, combination DMARDs may be appropriate following failed DMARD monotherapy.

All consultations provide opportunity for education, however we recommend that prior to commencing a new DMARD, a minimum of half an hour patient education is required.

Figure 6.1 Indications for disease-modifying drugs

	Rheumatoid arthritis	Psoriatic arthritis	Ankylosing spondylitis	SLE
Methotrexate	✔	✔	✔	
Metoject (s/c methotrexate)	✔	✔	✔	
Sulfasalazine	✔	✔		
Leflunomide	✔	✔		
Hydroxychloroquine	✔			✔

✔ Denotes use

✔ Denotes licensed indication

Methotrexate is commonly first choice DMARD. However the decision to commence methotrexate should be made taking into account co-existing co-morbidity and patient preference. Consider the patient's social history such as starting a family. Conception would not be advised and adequate contraception is necessary prior to commencement of treatment. Excess alcohol (over 22 units for men and 14 units for women) should be avoided. Patients must be aware that, prior to conception, methotrexate should be discontinued for three months.

6.2 Methotrexate

Mechanism of action

Methotrexate inhibits the metabolism of rapidly-dividing cells and is classed as an anti-metabolite drug. Methotrexate reduces folic acid required for DNA synthesis by binding to the site of dihydrofolate reductase.

Evidence grading

Grade A evidence. It is effective in controlling disease progression including radiographic damage and has a substantial clinical and statistical benefit for people with rheumatoid arthritis (Suarez-Almazor et al., 2000b).

Preparations

Tablets, subcutaneous injection, intra-muscular injection.

Dosage

Methotrexate may be given orally, or via intra-muscular or subcutaneous routes.

The dose range for oral methotrexate is a minimum dose of 7.5 mg weekly, usually with a maximum of 20 mg weekly. Local protocols may agree a maximum of 30 mg weekly.

The dose may be escalated by 2.5 mg fortnightly following review of disease activity until remission or maximum weekly dose achieved. Remission may be defined as no synovitis and/or a disease activity score (DAS) of < 2.6 (Luqmani et al., 2006). The DAS 28 is a validated tool to assess disease activity.

Be aware that only 2.5 mg tablets should be prescribed and dispensed. This prevents the potential for accidental overdose/error when using low dose methotrexate, as 10 mg tablets can be identical to 2.5 mg tablets. If acute methotrexate toxicity occurs, patients may require treatment with folinic acid.

Folic acid (5 mg weekly) is given, to be taken on day 3 post-methotrexate, and this may help to reduce the frequency of side effects.

If a patient is unable to tolerate oral methotrexate or disease activity remains uncontrolled consider using subcutaneous (s/c) route. Refer to Royal College of Nursing (RCN) guidance for teaching and administration of s/c methotrexate (www.rcn.org.uk).

Medac are now producing Metoject – methotrexate pre-filled syringes (intra-venous, intra-muscular, subcutaneous) 10 mg/ml for the treatment of rheumatoid arthritis – and these are available in five weekly dosage forms: 7.5 mg, 10 mg, 15 mg, 20 mg, 25 mg.

If your unit uses any other form of s/c methotrexate (7.5 mg – 25 mg) it is classed as a licensed preparation but an unlicensed route and a clinical management plan is required for a prescription to be legal. To prevent error, different dose volumes should be risk assessed prior to procurement.

Side effects

Nausea, rash, mouth ulcers, diarrhoea, headache, menstrual disturbance. Hepatic toxicity, myelosuppression, mucositis, pancytopenia and rarely interstitial pneumonitis (this can be fatal in 15 to 20 per cent of cases).

Cautions

Use with caution in the elderly. Use with extreme caution in patients with haematological depression, renal impairment, diarrhoea, and ulcerative disorders of the gastro-intestinal tract or high alcohol intake.

Contraindications

Hypersensitivity to any of the constituents. Significantly impaired renal or hepatic function. Pre-existing blood dyscrasias, such as significant marrow hypoplasia, leukopenia, thrombocytopenia or anaemia. Pregnancy and breast feeding.

Interactions

- Trimethoprim: can precipitate aplastic anaemia.

Check the BNF and SPC regularly for all reported side effects, contraindications and interactions.

- Penicillins and cephalosporins: increased toxicity of methotrexate (see Prescribing advice).
- Excretion of methotrexate probably reduced by NSAIDs, aspirin.
- Phenytoin has an additive anti-folate effect with methotrexate, and may also increase toxicity of methotrexate.
- Antimalarials increase anti-folate effect of methotrexate.
- Corticosteroids when given with methotrexate may increase risk of haematological toxicity.
- Probenecid: increased toxicity of methotrexate.
- Methotrexate may reduce absorption of digoxin.

Prescribing advice

We suggest folic acid is given to help reduce the frequency of side effects of methotrexate. Many variations of the co-prescribing of folic acid with methotrexate exist across rheumatology departments. Usually, 5 mg a day is given at least 24 hours after the methotrexate for one to three days. Folic acid should not be taken on the same day as methotrexate.

If prescribing trimethoprim, penicillins or cephalosporins (as no alternative), it is advisable to stop methotrexate for the duration of antibiotics. If a patient requires antibiotics and is systemically unwell, then methotrexate should be stopped for a minimum of one week. Live vaccines should be avoided (oral polio, MMR, yellow fever). Pneumococcal and annual influenza vaccine are recommended. Passive immunisation with varicella zoster immunoglobulin should be carried out in non-immune patients if exposed to chicken pox or shingles.

If a patient presents with acute shortness of breath while taking methotrexate (and up to four weeks after last dose), this raises the possibility of methotrexate pneumonitis and should be assessed urgently by a rheumatology or respiratory specialist. If in doubt stop the methotrexate. It is very important to warn the patient to report about the development of respiratory symptoms while they are taking methotrexate and this should be stressed during the education session prior to commencing methotrexate.

Pre-treatment assessment (BSR, 2007)

Full blood count (FBC), urea and electrolytes (U&E), liver function test (LFT) and chest X-ray (CXR) (unless CXR done within the last six months). Pulmonary function tests should be considered in selected patients.

Monitoring (BSR, 2007)

FBC, U&E and LFT every two weeks until dose of methotrexate and monitoring stable for a period of six weeks; monthly thereafter until the dose and disease is stable for a year.

Thereafter monitoring may be reduced in frequency, based on clinical judgement with due consideration of risk factors including age, co-morbidity and renal impairment which would necessitate continued monthly monitoring.

6.3 Sulfasalazine

Sulfasalazine is licensed for the treatment of rheumatoid arthritis, however the onset of effect can be slow and a marked effect may not be seen for six to 12 weeks.

Mechanism of action

Sulfasalazine is a combination of 5-amino salicylic acid (anti-inflammatory effect) and sulfapyridine (carrier molecules). The exact mechanism of action is unknown.

Evidence grading

Grade A evidence. It appears to have a clinically and statistically significant benefit on the disease activity of patients with rheumatoid arthritis. Its effects on overall health status and radiological progression would appear to be modest (Suarez-Almazor et al., 2000c).

Several studies indicate that sulfasalazine is effective in relieving the symptoms and slowing the progression of rheumatoid arthritis. Although it may show some effects within one month, it typically takes several months to be effective.

The decision to commence a DMARD such as sulfasalazine should be made taking into account co-existing co-morbidity and patient preference.

Preparations

Enteric-coated tablets (500 mg) and oral suspension (250 mg/ml).

> Check the BNF and SPC regularly for all reported side effects, contraindications and interactions.

Dosage

The dose is initially 500 mg daily increasing to 1 g twice a day over a 4-week period. Enteric-coated tablets should be used where there is gastro-intestinal intolerance.

Side effects

Nausea, rash, gastro-intestinal intolerance, bruising. Harmless side effects such as urine stained orange.

Some side effects may be dose-dependent and symptoms can sometimes be alleviated by reducing the dose.

Cautions

Pre-existing blood dyscrasias, such as significant marrow hypoplasia, leukopenia, thrombocytopenia or anaemia.

Contraindications

Where there is a significant hypersensitivity to sulfasalazine, sulfonamides or salicylates.

Interactions

Possibility that the uptake of digoxin and folate may be reduced.

Prescribing advice

Patients should be warned that it is not uncommon to develop an orange discoloration of their urine, and occasionally of their skin. This is a harmless side effect and should not cause alarm. The discoloration is temporary and disappears after stopping the medication. If a patient wears soft contact lenses, they may become stained. Sulfasalazine treatment is generally considered to be safe to use during pregnancy, however it may cause reversible azoospermia in men.

Pre-treatment assessment (BSR, 2007)

FBC, U&E and LFT.

Monitoring (BSR, 2007)

FBC and LFTs monthly for the first three months and three-monthly thereafter.

If, following the first year, dose and blood results remain stable, the frequency of blood tests can be reduced to every six months for the second year of treatment. Thereafter, monitoring may be discontinued.

The patient should be asked whether they have a rash or oral ulceration at each visit.

6.4 Leflunomide

Leflunomide is licensed for the treatment of rheumatoid arthritis and psoriatic arthritis. Improvement may be seen as soon as four to six weeks following commencement. Failure to tolerate methotrexate or sulfasalazine, and/or relevant co-existing co-morbidity and patient preference, would provide an indication for use. Consider patient's social history, such as whether they are starting a family. As for methotrexate, conception would not be advised and adequate contraception is necessary prior to commencement of treatment. If leflunomide is used in women of childbearing age, who wish to conceive later, contact the drug manufacturer for advice and support and they will advise the required drug washout and blood-testing procedures.

Be aware that the half life of leflunomide is lengthy. In the event of a serious side effect, stop leflunomide and consider washout therapy. Colestyramine is usually suggested. We suggest 8 g three times a day for 11 days for a full washout.

Blood pressure must be checked before commencing leflunomide treatment.

Mechanism of action

The active metabolite of leflunomide inhibits the human enzyme dihydroorotate dehydrogenase (DHODH) and exhibits anti-proliferative activity.

Evidence grading

Grade A evidence. Leflunomide appears to improve all clinical outcomes and delay radiographic progression at both six and 12 months of treatment

Check the BNF and SPC regularly for all reported side effects, contraindications and interactions.

compared to placebo. Its efficacy and adverse events at two years of treatment is comparable to sulfasalazine and methotrexate. Long-term efficacy and toxicity remains to be established (Osiri *et al.*, 2003).

Preparations

Tablets (10 mg, 20 mg, 100 mg).

Dosage

10 mg and 20 mg. The maintenance dose for rheumatoid arthritis and psoriatic arthritis is 10 mg to 20 mg once daily, depending on the severity (activity) of the disease. A loading dose of 100 mg daily for three days may be given initially.

Side effects

Nausea, diarrhoea, rash, pruritis, headache, gastro-intestinal intolerance, abdominal pain, alopecia and hypertension.

Cautions

Patients with impairment of liver function or moderate to severe renal insufficiency, impaired bone marrow function or significant anaemia, leucopenia, neutropenia or thrombocytopenia. History of tuberculosis.

Contraindications

Severe immunodeficiency disorder (AIDS), severe infection, severe hypoproteinaemia, for example in nephrotic syndrome. Pregnancy and breast feeding. Hypersensitivity to any of the tablet constituents.

Interactions

- May enhance anti-coagulant effect of warfarin.
- May enhance hypoglycaemic effect of tolbutamide.
- May increase the plasma concentration of phenytoin.

Prescribing advice

Start with 20 mg dose, reduce to 10 mg if significant side effects develop. Live vaccines should be avoided (oral polio, MMR and yellow fever). Pneumococcal and annual influenza vaccines are recommended. Excess alcohol should be avoided (more than 22 units for men and 14 units for women). Passive immunisation with varicella zoster immunoglobulin should be carried out in non-immune patients if exposed to chicken pox or shingles.

Contraception should be maintained for at least two years for women and three months for men after treatment discontinued or, alternatively, consider washout.

Recommended washout is colestyramine, 8 g administered three times a day usually for 11 days. Alternatively, 50 g of activated powdered charcoal may be administered four times a day.

Pre-treatment assessment (BSR, 2007)
- Full blood count (FBC) and liver function tests (LFTs).
- Check blood pressure. If > 140/90 mmHg on two consecutive readings two weeks apart, treat hypertension before commencing leflunomide.
- Check weight to allow assessment of weight loss that may be attributable to leflunomide.

Monitoring (BSR, 2007)
- FBC and LFTs every month for six months and, if stable, two-monthly thereafter.
- Continue to monitor FBC and LFT long-term monthly if co-prescribed with another immunosuppressant or potentially hepatotoxic agent.
- Blood pressure and weight should be checked at each monitoring visit.

6.5 Hydroxychloroquine

Hydroxychloroquine is an anti-malarial. Hydroxychloroquine can help relieve the symptoms and slow down the progression of rheumatoid arthritis. It is indicated for use in rheumatoid arthritis, juvenile chronic arthritis, discoid and systemic lupus erythematosus. Symptoms of rheumatoid arthritis should improve within six months.

Mechanism of action
Unknown.

Check the BNF and SPC regularly for all reported side effects, contraindications and interactions.

Chapter 6

Evidence grading

Grade A evidence for the treatment of rheumatoid arthritis (Suarez-Almazor *et al.*, 2000a). Overall effect appears to be moderate with a low toxicity profile. Its use in combination with other therapies is gaining acceptance (O'Dell *et al.*, 2002). It is used widely in systemic lupus erythematosus and Grade A evidence is available for its use during pregnancy in patients with systemic lupus erythematosus (Levy *et al.*, 2001; Williams *et al.*, 1994)

Preparations

Tablet (200 mg).

Dosage

Initially 400 mg daily in divided doses, with a maintenance dose of 200 mg–400 mg daily. Treatment should be discontinued if there is no improvement in rheumatoid arthritis by six months. Be aware of any local protocols for the use of hydroxychloroquine.

Side effects

Nausea, diarrhoea, headache, rarely visual changes or loss of vision, gastro-intestinal symptoms.

Cautions

Hepatic and renal impairment. Neurological disorders, severe gastro-intestinal disorders or porphyria. May exacerbate psoriasis and aggravate myasthenia gravis.

Contraindications

Known hypersensitivity, pre-existing maculopathy of the eye.

Interactions

- Has been reported to increase plasma digoxin levels.
- Absorption may be reduced by antacids.
- Amiodarone-increased risk of ventricular arrhythmias.

Prescribing advice

Enquire about any visual problems and suggest yearly visits to the optician.

Pre-treatment assessment (BSR, 2007)

- FBC, U&E, LFT.
- Ask about visual impairment (which is not corrected by glasses).
- Record near visual acuity of each eye (with reading glasses if worn) using a reading chart and if abnormality detected refer to optometrist.

Monitoring (BSR, 2007)

The Royal College of Ophthalmologists recommends an annual review either by an optometrist or the practitioner enquiring about visual symptoms, rechecking visual acuity and assessing for blurred vision using the reading chart.

Patients should be advised to report any visual disturbance. No blood monitoring is required.

Check the BNF and SPC regularly for all reported side effects, contraindications and interactions.

Biologic drugs

7.1 Overview

Biologic therapies are a treatment option for rheumatoid arthritis, psoriatic arthritis and ankylosing spondylitis. Cytokines, monoclonal antibodies and immunomodulators all have their own specific roles, clinical applications, mechanisms of action, and side effects. As biologic agents are approved and licensed for treatment, practitioners must know and understand the technology and mechanisms of action associated with these agents in conjunction with guidelines for prescribing safely.

The biologic agents etanercept, adalimumab and infliximab will be covered and their side effects, cautions, contraindications, interactions and prescribing advice for biologic agents are described together in Section 7.5. (Rituximab has not been covered in this edition as NICE approval for its use and indications is currently awaited.)

7.2 Etanercept

Etanercept is licensed as monotherapy or in combination with methotrexate for the treatment of moderate to severe active rheumatoid arthritis in adults where the response to disease-modifying anti-rheumatic drugs, including methotrexate (unless contraindicated), has been inadequate. It is also licensed for the treatment of active and progressive psoriatic arthritis in adults where the response to previous disease-modifying anti-rheumatic drug therapy has been inadequate and for active ankylosing spondylitis where there is an inadequate response to conventional therapy.

Mechanism of action

Etanercept is a human tumour necrosis factor receptor fusion protein produced by recombinant DNA technology. This combines with the cytokine tumour necrosis factor alpha and beta and prevents its action on the target cell.

Evidence grading

Grade A evidence for rheumatoid arthritis, psoriatic arthritis and ankylosing spondylitis (Chen *et al.*, 2006; van Riel *et al.*, 2006; Woolacott *et al.*, 2006; Zochling *et al.*, 2006).

Preparations

Dry powder vial for use as a subcutaneous injection, pre-filled syringe (25 mg, 50 mg).

Dosage

The recommended dose is 25 mg etanercept administered twice weekly or 50 mg administered once weekly by subcutaneous injection.

Side effects, cautions, contraindications, interactions and prescribing advice for biologic agents are described in Section 7.5

7.3 Adalimumab (Humira)

Humira is licensed in combination with methotrexate, or as monotherapy, for the treatment of moderate to severe, active rheumatoid arthritis in adult patients where the response to disease-modifying anti-rheumatic drugs including methotrexate has been inadequate. Adalimumab is also licensed for the treatment of active and progressive psoriatic arthritis in adults where the response to previous disease-modifying anti-rheumatic drug therapy has been inadequate, and for the treatment of adults with severe active ankylosing spondylitis who have had an inadequate response to conventional therapy.

Mechanism of action

Adalimumab is a recombinant human monoclonal antibody to tumour necrosis factor. It combines with soluble and membrane-bound tumour necrosis factor alpha and the complex is lysed (destroyed) by the immune system.

Evidence grading

Grade A evidence for rheumatoid arthritis (Breedveld *et al.*, 2006).

Preparations

Pre-filled syringe or pen (40 mg).

Dosage

The recommended dose is 40 mg adalimumab administered every other week as a single dose by subcutaneous injection. In those patients where there is an inadequate response, it may be increased to 40 mg weekly. Methotrexate is usually continued weekly during treatment

Side effects, cautions, contraindications, interactions and prescribing advice for biologic agents are described in Section 7.5.

7.4 Infliximab

Infliximab is licensed in combination with methotrexate for the treatment of moderate to severe, active rheumatoid arthritis in adult patients where the response to disease-modifying anti-rheumatic drugs has been inadequate. Infliximab is also licensed for the treatment of active and progressive psoriatic arthritis in adults where the response to previous disease-modifying anti-rheumatic drug therapy has been inadequate, and for the treatment of adults with severe active ankylosing spondylitis who have had an inadequate response to conventional therapy.

Mechanism of action

Infliximab is a chimeric IgG1 monoclonal antibody tumour necrosis factor which is partly of mouse (murine) origin. It combines with soluble and membrane-bound tumour necrosis factor alpha and the complex is lysed (destroyed) by the immune system.

Evidence grading

Grade A evidence for rheumatoid arthritis, psoriatic arthritis and ankylosing spondylitis (Chen *et al.*, 2006; Woolacott *et al.*, 2006; Zochling *et al.*, 2006).

Preparations

Intra-venous infusion dry powder vial (100 mg).

Chapter 7

Check the BNF and SPC regularly for all reported side effects, contraindications and interactions.

Dosage

For rheumatoid arthritis the dose is 3 mg/kg and for psoriatic arthritis and ankylosing spondylitis the dose is 5 mg/kg, given as an intravenous infusion over a two-hour period followed by infusions every six to eight weeks. The infusion can be administered over a one-hour period if there were no adverse events following the first three infusions. Methotrexate should be continued during treatment, or, if not tolerated or unsuitable, an alternative DMARD must be considered.

7.5 Side effects, cautions and contraindications

Side effects

Injection site reactions, nausea, abdominal pain, hypersensitivity reactions, headache, depression and Lupus-like syndrome.

Cautions

Active tuberculosis should be treated with standard treatment prior to commencement of biologics. Heart failure.

Contraindications

Sepsis or risk of sepsis and including chronic or localised infections. Pregnancy or breast feeding. Septic arthritis within last 12 months, sepsis of prosthetic joint within last 12 months. New York Heart Association (NYHA) Grade 3–4 congestive cardiac failure for infliximab and adalimumab. Clear history of demyelinating disease. Previous tuberculosis. Hypersensitivity to any of the constituents.

Interactions

None reported. Avoid live vaccines.

Prescribing advice

If exposed to significant herpes zoster virus the patient should seek urgent medical attention. Passive immunisation with varicella zoster immunoglobulin may be required. Patients must fulfil the British Society for Rheumatology criteria prior to commencement of a biologic.

Patients with rheumatoid arthritis must:

- fulfil American College of Rheumatology 1987 classification for rheumatoid arthritis.
- have active rheumatoid arthritis (DAS 28 > 5.1) on two occasions, one month apart.
- fail standard therapy defined as failure to respond (treatment for six months) or tolerate two standard DMARDs. One of those failed or not tolerated must be methotrexate.

Discontinuation would apply if:

- there was a failure to respond after three months of treatment (DAS 28 to improve by > 1.2 or to reduce to < 3.2) or the development of severe adverse effect.

For patients with ankylosing spondylitis, active spinal disease is defined as:

- BASDAI (Bath AS disease activity index) = or > 4cms
- Spinal pain VAS (visual analogue scale) = or > 4cms

taken at least four weeks apart.

Discontinuation would apply if:

- there was no improvement in BASDAI or spinal pain VAS or the development of a severe adverse effect.

For patients with psoriatic arthritis, use the Psoriatic Arthritis Response Criteria (PsARC) test which comprises the following four measures:

- patient global assessment (0–5 Likert scale)
- physician global assessment (0–5 Likert scale) with improvement defined as a decrease by at least one unit, and worsening defined as an increase by at least one unit
- tender joint score with improvement defined as a decrease of at least 30 per cent and worsening defined as an increase of at least 30 per cent
- swollen joint score with improvement defined as a decrease of at least 30 per cent and worsening defined as an increase of at least 30 per cent.

Check the BNF and SPC regularly for all reported side effects, contraindications and interactions.

Chapter 7

Patient must also:

- have peripheral arthritis with three or more tender joints and three or more swollen joints.
- have failed adequate trial of at least two DMARDs, either individually or in combination.

Discontinuation would apply if:

- there was a failure to improve two of the PsARC test factors, one of which being the joint tenderness or swelling score, with no worsening in any of the four criteria.
- there was a development of a severe adverse effect or event.

Osteoporosis

8.1 Overview

Patients who have had a fragility fracture, are on corticosteroids, or are at risk of osteoporosis from any other cause should be assessed and treated according to the current National Institute for Health and Clinical Excellence (NICE) and Royal College of Physicians guidance (see www. nice.org.uk and RCP, 2002).

Bisphosphonates are the first choice drugs for osteoporosis treatment; strontium ranelate, raloxifene, teriparatide and calcium and vitamin D supplementation will also be covered in this chapter. HRT is not licensed for use as treatment for osteoporosis and therefore will not be covered.

8.2 Bisphosphonates

General prescribing points

Bisphosphonates are very poorly absorbed from the gastro-intestinal tract. Correct dosing and administration of these preparations is key to achieving their effect.

- A bisphosphonate is best taken immediately after getting up in the morning on an empty stomach.
- Patients should be advised to take alendronic acid, ibandronic acid or risedronate sodium with a full glass of tap water and should not lie down for at least 30 minutes after taking their tablet.
- Use of these preparations may be ineffective due to non-compliance with the correct regime. In apparent non-responders, check that patients are taking the medicine correctly.
- Food and other drugs should not be taken for 30 minutes to one hour after taking tablet.
- Use with caution in renal impairment (see the individual drugs for more information).

- If calcium is required on the same day this should be taken with a main meal later in the day.

Mechanism of action

All the bisphosphonates prevent the breakdown of bone by osteoclasts.

Interactions

Other than the potential for interference with absorption (most notable with some foods, calcium and iron), there are no known drug interactions.

Alendronic acid

All doses are licensed for use in post-menopausal women. Only 5 mg/day and 10 mg/day have a license for male use. Only the 5 mg/day dose is licensed for pre-menopausal women.

Evidence grading

Grade A evidence in fracture reduction for vertebral and non-vertebral sites (Liberman *et al.*, 2006).

Preparations

Tablets (5 mg, 10 mg or 70 mg).

Dosage

Treatment of post-menopausal women: 10 mg daily or 70 mg once weekly. Treatment of osteoporosis in men: 10 mg/day. Prevention of post-menopausal osteoporosis: 5 mg/day. Prevention and treatment of corticosteroid-induced osteoporosis in pre-menopausal women and men: 5 mg/day, and 10 mg/day if post-menopausal and not on HRT.

Side effects

Oesophagitis, dysphagia, abdominal pain and distension, diarrhoea or constipation, flatulence, musculoskeletal pain, headache, rash, erythema, photosensitivity, uveitis, transient decrease in serum phosphate, nausea, vomiting, peptic ulceration and hypersensitivity reactions also reported. Osteonecrosis of the jaw.

Cautions

Upper gastro-intestinal disorders (dysphagia, symptomatic oesophageal disease, gastritis, duodenitis or ulcers). History (within one year) of ulcers, active gastro-intestinal bleeding or surgery of the upper gastro-intestinal tract, renal impairment (avoid if creatinine clearance < 35 ml/min). Correct disturbances of calcium and mineral metabolism (for example, vitamin D deficiency, hypocalcaemia) before starting bisphosphonates.

Contraindications

Abnormalities of the oesophagus and other factors which delay emptying (for example, stricture or achalasia), hypocalcaemia, pregnancy or breast feeding. Hypersensitivity to any of the tablet constituents.

Prescribing advice

Alendronic acid should be given with adequate calcium and vitamin D ingestion and, in most instances, calcium supplements would be required. Trials used 500 mg of calcium supplements and 250 IU of vitamin D per day. Patients should be advised to stop taking the tablets and refer to the doctor if they develop symptoms of oesophageal irritation such as dysphagia, new or worsening heartburn, pain on swallowing, or retrosternal pain.

Alendronic acid is also available as a 70 mg tablet, which is taken once a week, on the same day each week.

Disodium etidronate and calcium (Didronel PMO)

Disodium etidronate must be used as part of a cyclical regime. This is because osteomalacia has been reported with its continuous use in Paget's Disease. Efficacy is only significant if taken for more than 12 months. Licensed for treatment of osteoporosis and prevention of bone loss in post-menopausal women and treatment and prevention of glucocorticoid-induced osteoporosis.

Evidence grading

Grade A evidence for reduction of vertebral fractures, Grade B for non-vertebral fractures (Cranney et al., 2001).

Preparation

Tablets (200 mg and 400 mg), Didronel PMO pack.

Dosage

400 mg for 14 days followed by 76 days of 1.25 g calcium carbonate.

Chapter 8

Check the BNF and SPC regularly for all reported side effects, contraindications and interactions.

Side effects

Nausea, diarrhoea or constipation, abdominal pain, skin reactions, transient hyperphosphataemia, headache, parasthesia, peripheral neuropathy, blood disorders (including leucopenia, agranulocytosis and pancytopenia), osteonecrosis of the jaw.

Cautions

Reduce dose in mild renal impairment.

Contraindications

Moderate to severe renal impairment, pregnancy and breast feeding. Cacit component is not indicated for osteoporosis in presence of hypercalcaemia or hypercalciuria. Hypersensitivity to any of the tablet constituents.

Prescribing advice

It is marketed as a calendar pack (Didronel PMO) containing disodium etidronate 400 mg once daily for 14 days then calcium carbonate 1.25g (Cacit) once daily for 76 days, repeated as a 90-day cycle. The disodium etidronate is the important part of the regime. The Cacit, if not tolerated, can be replaced by another calcium supplement.

Counsel the patient to avoid food for at least two hours before and after the disodium etidronate tablets in the cycle, particularly calcium-containing products such as milk; also to avoid iron and mineral supplements and antacids.

Risedronate sodium

Licensed for treatment of post-menopausal osteoporosis to reduce risk of hip or vertebral fracture, prevention of corticosteroid-induced osteoporosis and prevention of osteoporosis in post-menopausal women.

Evidence grading

Grade A evidence in vertebral and non-vertebral fracture reduction (Liberman *et al.*, 2006).

Preparations

Tablets (5 mg, 35 mg).

Dosage

Treatment or prevention of osteoporosis (including corticosteroid-induced) in post-menopausal women: 5 mg daily. Treatment of post-menopausal osteoporosis: 35 mg once weekly.

Side effects

Upper gastro-intestinal symptoms – dyspepsia, nausea, diarrhoea, constipation, oesophageal stricture, and duodenitis; headache, musculo-skeletal pain.

Cautions

Oesophageal abnormalities and other factors which delay transit or emptying (for example, stricture and achalasia). Renal impairment – avoid if creatinine clearance is < 30 ml/min. Correct disturbances of calcium and mineral metabolism before starting.

Contraindications

Hypocalcaemia, pregnancy and breast feeding.

Prescribing advice

Reinforce the importance of taking bisphosphonates correctly or they will be ineffective.

Ibandronic acid

Ibandronic acid may be taken daily, but it is the only oral bisphosphonate that is approved to be taken monthly. Ibandronic acid is licensed to prevent and to treat osteoporosis in post-menopausal women.

Evidence grading

Grade A evidence for reduction of vertebral fractures with daily preparation (Felsenberg *et al.*, 2005).

Preparations

Tablets (2.5 mg and 150 mg), intra-venous injection (3 mg/3 ml).

Chapter 8

Check the BNF and SPC regularly for all reported side effects, contraindications and interactions.

Dosage

The dose of ibandronic acid tablets is 2.5 mg daily or 150 mg once monthly. The intra-venous dose is 3 mg every three months.

Side effects

Flu-like symptoms (monthly preparation), musculoskeletal pain, dyspepsia, abdominal pain and diarrhoea.

Cautions

Renal impairment.

Contraindications

Creatinine clearance < 30ml/min, hypocalcaemia, pregnancy and breast feeding. Hypersensitivity to any of the tablet constituents.

Prescribing advice

If monthly dosing is used, the tablet should be taken on the same day of each month. Tablets should be taken at least 60 minutes before the first food or drink of the day (other than plain water) or before other oral medication, because of concern that food or medication will interfere with the absorption of ibandronic acid. Tablets should not be chewed or sucked in order to avoid irritation of the mouth and throat.

8.3 Strontium ranelate

Licensed for the treatment of post-menopausal osteoporosis to reduce the risk of vertebral and hip fractures.

Mechanism of action

It is thought to have a dual effect on bone metabolism, increasing bone formation and decreasing bone resorption.

Evidence grading

Grade A evidence for vertebral and non-vertebral fracture reduction, Grade B for hip fracture reduction (Stevenson et al., 2007).

Preparations

Sachet (2 g).

Dosage

The recommended dose is one 2 g sachet once daily, taken as a suspension in water, two hours before eating.

Side effects

Nausea, diarrhoea, headache, dermatitis and creatinine kinase elevations. A serious adverse event associated with strontium ranelate therapy is an increased incidence of venous thromboembolism and pulmonary embolism.

Cautions

In patients at increased risk of venous thromboembolism.

Contraindications

Severe renal impairment (creatinine clearance < 30 ml/min), hypersensitivity, pregnancy and breast feeding.

Interactions

May prevent absorption of oral tetracycline or quinolone antibiotics

Prescribing advice

This is an alternative treatment option for women for whom bisphosphonates are contraindicated, or who are unable to comply with the special recommendations for use of bisphosphonates, or who cannot take them because of intolerance. The absorption of strontium ranelate is reduced by food, milk and derivative products. It should therefore be administered between meals, ideally at bedtime and preferably at least two hours before and after eating.

8.4 Teriparatide

Prescribe according to National Institute for Health and Clinical Excellence (NICE) guidance (www.nice.org.uk). At the time of going to press this is women over 65 years of age with further fracture despite bisphosphonate or intolerance to bisphosphonate, combined with extremely low bone mineral density or very low bone density with two or more fractures and other risk factors for osteoporosis.

Check the BNF and SPC regularly for all reported side effects, contraindications and interactions.

Mechanism of action

Teriparatide is a synthetic version of human parathyroid hormone, which is produced by the parathyroid glands. This hormone is involved in the metabolism of calcium and phosphorus. Teriparatide mimics the effects of the natural human hormone and is used to increase bone formation by direct effects on osteoblasts, indirectly increasing the intestinal absorption of calcium, increasing the tubular re-absorption of calcium and excretion of phosphate by the kidney.

Evidence grading

Grade A evidence for vertebral and non-vertebral fracture reduction in post-menopausal women with previous fractures (Cranney *et al.*, 2006).

Preparation

Injection (250 micrograms/ml 3ml pre-filled pen intended for 28 doses).

Dosage

20 micrograms once daily by subcutaneous injection.

Side effects

Pain, swelling, redness, bruising or itching around injection site, limb pain, nausea and vomiting, dizziness, headache, fatigue, depression, chest pain, muscle cramps, vertigo, dyspnoea, raised cholesterol levels, increased sweating, anaemia, asthenia, palpitations, sciatica, hypotension, gastro-oesophageal reflux, polyuria, weight gain.

Cautions

Moderate renal impairment, people who have or have recently had stones in the urinary tract.

Contraindications

Severe renal impairment, metabolic bone diseases other than osteoporosis e.g. Paget's Disease of bone, hyperparathyroidism, hypercalcaemia, bone cancer, previous radiotherapy to the bones, unexplained raised levels of alkaline phosphatase, pregnancy, breast feeding. Hypersensitivity to any of the constituents.

Interactions

- Digoxin, as teriparatide, causes temporary increases in the blood level of calcium and this may potentially predispose people to side effects associated with digoxin.

Prescribing advice

In short-term clinical studies with teriparatide, isolated episodes of transient orthostatic hypotension were observed. Typically, an event began within four hours of dosing and spontaneously resolved within a few minutes to a few hours. When transient orthostatic hypotension occurred, it happened within the first several doses, was relieved by placing subjects in a reclining position and did not preclude continued treatment.

8.5 Raloxifene

Raloxifene is licensed for the prevention and treatment of osteoporosis in post-menopausal women. It is not indicated for the treatment of menopausal symptoms.

Mechanism of action

Raloxifene is a selective oestrogen receptor modulator (SERM) which has an agonist effect on bone.

Evidence grading

Grade A evidence for vertebral fracture reduction (Seeman *et al.*, 2006) in post-menopausal women.

Preparation

Tablet (60 mg).

Dosage

60 mg once daily.

Side effects

Venous thrombo-embolism, thrombo-phlebitis. It should not be used within one year of the menopause because of an increased incidence of

Check the BNF and SPC regularly for all reported side effects, contraindications and interactions.

vasomotor symptoms. Other side effects include leg cramps, peripheral oedema, flu-like symptoms.

Cautions

Risk factors for venous thrombo-embolism, active breast cancer (avoid use).

Contraindications

History of venous thromboembolism, undiagnosed uterine bleeding, endometrial cancer, liver impairment, cholestasis, severe renal impairment, pregnancy and breast feeding. Hypersensitivity to any of the tablet constituents.

Interactions

- Colestyramine (or other anion exchange resins) which significantly reduces the absorption and enterohepatic cycling of raloxifene.
- Anticoagulant effect of warfarin antagonised.

Prescribing advice

This preparation is most suitable for preventing osteoporosis in women who are considering alternative therapy to HRT, for example those concerned about breast cancer risk with HRT, patients who have no menopausal symptoms at least 12 months after their last period and those at an increased cardiovascular risk.

It is also an alternative to bisphosphonates without the compliance issues.

8.6 Calcium with or without vitamin D supplements

Licensed to be an adjunct to conventional therapy in the prevention and treatment of osteoporosis.

Mechanism of action

Supplement for when dietary intake is insufficient.

Evidence grading

Grade A evidence that calcium supplementation will result in increased bone mass (Shea *et al.*, 2002), particularly in patients with an inadequate dietary intake.

Preparations

Tablets, effervescent tablets, chewable tablets, granules, powder and syrup (various strengths).

Dosage

Supplements should aim to achieve a total intake of 1200–1500 mg elemental calcium a day (usually 1–2 tablets).

Side effects

Constipation, flatulence, nausea, abdominal pain and diarrhoea – usually mild.

Cautions

Renal impairment, sarcoidosis, pregnancy and breast feeding.

Contraindications

Conditions associated with hypercalcaemia and hypercalciuria. Hypersensitivity to any of the tablet constituents.

Interactions

- Thiazide diuretics reduce the urinary excretion of calcium. Due to increased risk of hypercalcaemia, serum calcium should be regularly monitored during concomitant use of thiazide diuretics.

- Systemic corticosteroids reduce calcium absorption. During concomitant use, it may be necessary to increase the dose.

- Tetracycline preparations should be administered at least two hours before, or four to six hours after, oral intake of calcium.

- Hypercalcaemia may increase the toxicity of digoxin during treatment with calcium.

- If a bisphosphonate or sodium fluoride is used concomitantly, this preparation should be administered at least three hours before the

Check the BNF and SPC regularly for all reported side effects, contraindications and interactions.

intake of Calcichew Forte chewable tablets since gastro-intestinal absorption may be reduced.

- Oxalic acid (found in spinach and rhubarb) and phytic acid (found in whole cereals) may inhibit calcium absorption through formation of insoluble calcium salts. The patient should not take calcium products within two hours of eating foods high in oxalic acid and phytic acid.

- Absorption of levothyroxine, iron and zinc reduced by calcium salts.

Prescribing advice

For patients who lack adequate exposure to the sun (which includes most elderly patients for eight months of the year) or who have inadequate diet, or some degree of renal impairment, it may be necessary to provide vitamin D 400–800 IU daily. Elderly patients are at greatest risk and are likely to need Adcal-D3 or Calcichew D3 Forte 2 tablets daily. Some of these patients with renal impairment will not be able to 1-hydroxylate vitamin D and will benefit from treatment with calcium 500 mg daily and 1 alpha Calcidol 250 nanograms daily.

Monitoring

Ideally treatment should be monitored, by measuring plasma calcium levels.

Allopurinol, colchicine and viscosupplementation

9.1 Allopurinol

Allopurinol is used to prevent recurrent attacks of gout. It is not a treatment for acute gout.

Mechanism of action

Allopurinol is an isomer of hypoxanthine and inhibits the production of uric acid, the metabolite which causes gout, by inhibiting the enzyme xanthine oxidase. Allopurinol is rapidly metabolised to oxipurinol which is also a xanthine oxidase inhibitor.

Evidence grading

Grade A evidence for treatment of gout (Zhang *et al.*, 2006).

Preparations

Tablets (100 mg and 300 mg).

Dosage

100–600 mg daily.

Side effects

Rash, Stevens Johnson syndrome, hypersensitivity consisting of fever, eosinophilia and hepatitis, deterioration in renal function, nausea and vomiting, vertigo.

Cautions

Reduced doses should be used in patients with hepatic or renal impairment.

Contraindications

Hypersensitivity to allopurinol.

Interactions

- Azathioprine is metabolised to 6-mercaptopurine which is inactivated by the action of xanthine oxidase. Only 25 per cent of the usual dose of 6-mercaptopurine or azathioprine should be given.

- Vidarabine (adenine arabinoside): The plasma half-life of vidarabine is increased in the presence of allopurinol.

- Chlorpropamide: increased risk of prolonged hypoglycaemic activity because allopurinol and chlorpropamide may compete for excretion in the renal tubule, particularly if renal function is poor.

- Increased effect of warfarin and other coumarin anti-coagulants when co-administered with allopurinol.

- Theophylline: inhibition of the metabolism of theophylline may occur.

- Ampicillin/Amoxicillin: an increase in incidence of skin rash can occur with concurrent use of allopurinol.

- Ciclosporin: plasma concentration of ciclosporin may be increased.

- Didanosine: a dose reduction of didanosine may be needed.

Prescribing advice

Start once the acute attack has settled or with NSAID/colchicine cover (500 micrograms twice daily). Serum urate level should respond after four weeks' treatment with allopurinol. It takes six months to see full effects and gouty tophi reduction may take years. If gout is difficult to control, check patient's compliance.

In patients without significant co-morbidity or renal impairment, start at 300 mg, check plasma urate levels at four weeks and increase in 100 mg doses until urate in normal range.

In patients with renal impairment, start at 100 mg and increase in 100 mg increments.

Allopurinol should be taken orally once a day after a meal. If the daily dosage exceeds 300 mg and gastro-intestinal side effects occur, dividing the dose may control the problem.

9.2 Colchicine

Colchicine is licensed for use in acute gout and to prevent recurrent attacks.

Mechanism of action

It reduces the inflammatory response to urate crystals, by possibly inhibiting the migration of granulocytes into the inflamed area.

Evidence grading

Grade A evidence for treatment of acute gout (Schlesinger *et al.*, 2006).

Preparations

Tablets (500 micrograms). Colchicine can also be given intra-venously.

Dosage

Acute gout: 1 mg initially then 500 micrograms every two to three hours until pain is relieved or diarrhoea or vomiting occurs, or until a total dose of 6 mg is reached. Do not repeat the course of treatment within 3 days. For prophylaxis: 500 micrograms two to three times daily.

Side effects

The most common side effects of colchicine involve the stomach and bowel and are dose related. Common side effects include nausea, vomiting, diarrhoea and abdominal pain. Larger doses may cause profuse diarrhoea, gastro-intestinal haemorrhage, muscle weakness, skin rashes, renal and hepatic damage. Alopecia, peripheral neuritis and bone marrow depression with agranulocytosis and aplastic anaemia may occur after prolonged treatment.

Cautions

Where profuse diarrhoea may cause serious compromise, for example in elderly or debilitated patients or those with cardiac, renal, hepatic or gastro-intestinal disease.

Contraindications

History of hypersensitivity to colchicine. Blood dyscrasias. Pregnancy and breast feeding.

Check the BNF and SPC regularly for all reported side effects, contraindications and interactions.

Chapter 9

Interactions

- Colchicine may impair the absorption of vitamin B12.

- May induce muscle disorders when used in combination with ciclosporin.

- Erythromycin, clarithromycin or tolbutamide may lead to colchicine toxicity.

Prescribing advice

In those patients with gout where NSAIDs are contraindicated (see Chapter 5) colchicine can used. This drug frequently produces abdominal pain and diarrhoea which can be extremely difficult for the patient if the gout is limiting mobility already. These side effects are very prone to occur if the SPC dosage regime is used. Those people that tolerate colchicine learn to take it as soon as the episode starts and sometimes manage to use as little as a 500 micrograms twice-daily regime through the attack. Colchicine should be taken with food.

Monitoring

All patients taking colchicine long-term require full blood count monitoring.

9.3 Viscosupplementation

Several preparations of sodium hyaluronate (Arthrease, Durolane, Fermathron, Hyalgan, Orthovisc, Ostenil, Suplasyn) and its derivative hylan G-F 20 (Synvisc) are available, all highly viscous but differing in molecular weight and degree of polymerisation. Many are licensed as a medical device and not as a drug. They are licensed for use in knee osteo-arthritis and given by intra-articular injection. Increasingly manufacturers are looking to reduce the number of injections needed and trying to dem-onstrate effectiveness in other joints.

Mechanism of action

Uncertain. Endogenous hyaluronic acid provides viscosity and elasticity to synovial fluid, however all the exogenous preparations are removed in days. Studies show benefit from six weeks to six months after injection so another mechanism is needed to explain its action. This may be explained by exogenous hyaluronic acid interacting with various components of the synovial cavity (synoviocytes and chondrocytes).

Evidence grading

Grade A evidence (Bellamy *et al.*, 2006) for osteoarthritic knees.

Preparation

Various injections.

Dosages

Hyalgan: 20 mg/2ml in three injections (one a week)

Orthovisc: 30 mg/2ml in three injections (one a week)

Side effects

Pain, swelling, effusion, heat and redness may rarely occur at the injection site.

Contraindications

Hypersensitivity to hyaluronates, birds or bird products. General contraindications to performing a joint injection.

Prescribing advice

Aspirate joint effusion prior to injection of viscosupplement. Patients are advised to rest for the first 48 hours and avoid weight bearing where possible, with a gradual return to their normal level of activity. Symptoms should improve after five to 13 weeks. The manufacturers state that visco-supplements should not be repeated within a six month period.

Check the BNF and SPC regularly for all reported side effects, contraindications and interactions.

Corticosteroids

Corticosteroids used for rheumatological conditions may be in the form of oral prednisolone, intra-muscular or intra-articular methylprednisolone, hydrocortisone or triamcinolone.

When using corticosteroids, be aware that the lowest possible dose for the shortest amount of time will minimise the risks of side effects, particularly osteoporosis. For this reason parenteral corticosteroids are often used instead of oral corticosteroids.

After receiving regular corticosteroids for three weeks adrenal suppression occurs, and, in such a situation, if the corticosteroids are stopped abruptly, collapse or death from adrenal insufficiency can occur. (Refer to BNF for most recent guidance.)

During times of physical stress increased corticosteroid may be needed and regular corticosteroid may suppress the appropriate response. It is important to increase corticosteroids in that situation.

Mechanism of action

The precise mechanism by which corticosteroids suppress inflammation is unknown.

Evidence grading

Grade A evidence for oral steroid therapy in establishing control of synovitis and reducing erosion development (Gotzsche & Johansen, 2003; Jones *et al.*, 2003).

Grade A evidence for intra-muscular methylprednisolone controlling synovitis while awaiting effects of gold therapy in rheumatoid arthritis (Choy *et al.*, 1993; Corkill *et al.*, 1990).

Grade A evidence for intra-venous methylprednisolone controlling synovitis while awaiting effects of methotrexate therapy in rheumatoid arthritis (van der Veen & Bijlsma, 1993).

Preparations

Tablets, intra-muscular injection, intra-venous, intra-articular or intra-synovial injection.

Dosage

- Oral prednisolone: 2.5 mg (brown), 5 mg (red) or 1 mg (white)
- Soluble prednisolone tablets: 5 mg
- Intra-muscular methylprednisolone: 40 mg/ml
- Intra-articular methylprednisolone or triamcinolone: 40 mg/ml
- Intra-venous methylprednisolone: 1g on three alternate or consecutive days.
- Intra-synovial hydrocortisone: 25 mg/ml

Figure 10.1 Suggested doses when prescribing corticosteroids

Indication	Oral prednisolone indication	Oral dose range adapted from the BNF (2006)
Polymyalgia rheumatica (PMR) and giant cell arteritis (GCA)	✔ ✔	10–15 mg daily initially (reduction to 7.5 mg for maintenance) 40–60 mg initially followed by maintenance dose of 7.5 mg–10 mg daily
Vasculitis polymyositis	✔	60 mg initially followed by maintenance dose of 10–15 mg daily
Rheumatoid arthritis	✔	7.5 mg initially, for no longer than 2–4 years

Intra-articular methylprednisolone (Depomedrone) or triamcinolone (Kenalog) is indicated for local inflammation of joints and soft tissues. Typically 40 mg is used for medium-sized joints and 10–20 mg for small joints or tendons. For superficial soft tissue injections, for example for lateral epicondylitis, hydrocortisone is used to minimise the risk of skin atrophy.

Intra-muscular methylprednisolone (Depomedrone) is not licensed for control of symptoms in inflammatory arthritis. In this instance to prescribe would require a clinical management plan, a patient group direction or an off-label prescription.

Intra-venous methylprednisolone may be used in rheumatology units for an acute flare of inflammatory arthritis or induction of remission of vasculitis. It is given to suppress inflammation where lower doses of corticosteroids have not been effective. It is particularly important to screen and treat infection prior to giving the methylprednisolone in this form.

Side effects
- Gastro-intestinal – dyspepsia, peptic ulceration, nausea
- Musculoskeletal – proximal myopathy, osteoporosis, avascular necrosis
- Endocrine – adrenal suppression, weight gain, increased appetite
- Ophthalmic – glaucoma, corneal or scleral thinning
- Neuropsychiatric effects – euphoria, depression, psychosis
- Other effects – bruising, striae, impaired healing, skin atrophy.

Cautions
Caution is necessary when oral prednisolone is prescribed for patients with a previous history of tuberculosis or X-ray changes characteristic of tuberculosis. Hypertension, congestive heart failure, liver failure, renal insufficiency, diabetes mellitus or osteoporosis. A history of severe affective disorders and particularly those with a previous history of steroid-induced psychoses, epilepsy or seizure disorders, peptic ulceration.

Be aware that suppression of the inflammatory response and immune function increases the susceptibility to infections and their severity. In addition serious infection such as septicaemia and tuberculosis may be masked in patients taking prednisolone.

Contraindications
Systemic infections.

Check the BNF and SPC regularly for all reported side effects, contraindications and interactions.

Interactions

- Drugs such as anti-convulsants, phenytoin and carbamazepine, and rifampicin, rifabutin, and primidone may reduce the therapeutic efficacy of prednisolone and other corticosteroids by increasing the rate of metabolism.

- Patients with diabetes mellitus receiving insulin and/or oral hypoglycaemic agents may require dosage adjustments to such therapy.

- Salicylates and prednisolone should be used concurrently with caution and patients receiving both drugs must be observed closely for adverse effects of either drug.

- Erythromycin inhibits metabolism of methylprednisolone and possibly other corticosteroids.

- Response to anti-coagulants may be reduced or occasionally enhanced by corticosteroids and close monitoring of the INR is required.

Prescribing advice

If the patient is going to be referred on to secondary care then discuss initiation of regular corticosteroids with the specialist team, first, as clinical, serological and histopathological signs of inflammation will rapidly disappear.

Patients should be advised to carry steroid treatment cards if they receive oral corticosteroids. These cards provide guidance on the precautions to be taken to minimise risk and provide details of prescriber, drug, dosage and duration of treatment.

If a patient is anticipated to be receiving a three-month or more course of prednisolone (irrespective of dose) then the Royal College of Physicians guidance on preventing corticosteroid-induced osteoporosis should be followed (RCP, 2002).

Be aware that chicken pox, although normally a minor illness, may be fatal in immunosuppressed patients. Patients without a clear medical history of chicken pox should be advised to avoid close personal contact with chicken pox or herpes zoster and, if exposed, they should seek urgent medical attention. Passive immunisation with varicella zoster immunoglobulin is required for non-immune patients within ten days of exposure to chicken pox, who are receiving prednisolone or other corticosteroids, or who have taken them within the previous three months. If a diagnosis of chicken pox is confirmed, prednisolone should not be stopped and the dose may need to be increased.

Chapter 10

84

Patients should also be advised to avoid exposure to measles if possible and, if necessary, to seek immediate medical assistance should exposure occur. Intra-muscular immunoglobulin prophylaxis may be required.

Check the BNF and SPC regularly for all reported side effects, contraindications and interactions.

References

Arnold, L.M., Rosen, A., Pritchett, Y.L., D'Souza, D.N., Goldstein, D.J., Iyengar, S. and Wernicke, J.F. (2005). A randomized, double-blind, placebo-controlled trial of duloxetine in the treatment of women with fibromyalgia with or without major depressive disorder. *Pain*, **119**(1–3), 5–15.

Barber, N., Parsons, J., Clifford, S., Darracott, R. and Horne, R. (2004). Patients' problems with new medication for chronic conditions. *Quality and Safety in Health Care*, **13**, 172–175.

Barden, J., Edwards, J., Moore, A. and McQuay, H. (2004). Single dose oral paracetamol (acetaminophen) for post-operative pain (Cochrane Review). *The Cochrane Library*, **1**.

Bellamy, N., Campbell, J., Robinson, V., Gee, T., Bourne, R. and Wells, G. (2006). Viscosupplementation for the treatment of osteoarthritis of the knee (Cochrane Review). *The Cochrane Library*, **2**.

Bennett, R.M., Kamin, M., Karim, R. and Rosenthal, N. (2003). Tramadol and acetaminophen combination tablets in the treatment of fibromyalgia pain: a double-blind, randomized, placebo-controlled study. *American Journal of Medicine*, **114**(7), 537–545.

Breedveld, F.C., Weisman, M.H., Kavanaugh, A.F., Cohen, S.B., Pavelka, K., van Vollenhoven, R., Sharp, J., Perez, J.L. and Spencer-Green, G.T. (2006). The PREMIER study: A multicenter, randomized, double-blind clinical trial of combination therapy with adalimumab plus methotrexate versus methotrexate alone or adalimumab alone in patients with early, aggressive rheumatoid arthritis who had not had previous methotrexate treatment. *Arthritis & Rheumatism*, **54**(1), 26–37.

British Society for Rheumatology (BSR) (2007). BSR/BHPR DMARD Guideline Group (May 2007). Protocol for monitoring bloods and urine of patients with rheumatoid arthritis taking DMARDs. Available at www.rheumatology.org.uk.

Caulfield, H. (2004). Responsibility, accountability and liability in nurse prescribing 2004. *Prescribing Nurse*, **2**(2), 18–21.

Chen, Y.F., Jobanputra, P., Barton, P., Jowett, S., Bryan, S., Clark, W., Fry-Smith, A. and Burls, A. (2006). A systematic review of the effectiveness of adalimumab, etanercept and infliximab for the treatment of rheumatoid arthritis in adults and an economic evaluation of their cost-effectiveness. *Health Technology Assessment*, **10**(42), 1–248.

Choy, E.H., Kingsley, G.H., Corkill, M.M. and Panayi, G.S. (1993). Intra-muscular methylprednisolone is superior to pulse oral methylprednisolone during the induction phase of chrysotherapy. *British Journal of Rheumatology*, **32**(8), 734–739.

Cobra, C.J., Cobra, J.F. and Cobra, N.C. (1983). Use of piroxicam in the treatment of acute gout. *European Journal of Rheumatology and Inflammation*, **6**(1), 126–133.

Collantes, E., Curtis, S.P., Lee, K.W., Casas, N., McCarthy, T., Melian, A., Zhao, P.L., Rodgers, D.B., McCormick, C.L., Lee, M., Lines, C.R. and Gertz, B.J. (2002). A multinational randomized, controlled, clinical trial of etoricoxib in the treatment of rheumatoid arthritis. *BMC Family Practice*, **3**(10), 3–10.

Corkill, M.M., Kirkham, B.W., Chikanza, I.C., Gibson, T. and Panayi, G.S. (1990). Intra-muscular depot methylprednisolone induction of chrysotherapy in rheumatoid arthritis: a 24-week randomized controlled trial. *British Journal of Rheumatology*, **29**(4), 274–279.

Cranney, A., Guyatt, G., Krolicki, N., Welch, V., Griffith, L., Adachi, J.D., Shea, B., Tugwell, P. and Wells, G. (2001). A meta-analysis of etidronate for the treatment of post-menopausal osteoporosis. *Osteoporosis International*, **12**(2), 140–151.

de Craen, A.J., Di Giulio, G., Lampe-Schoenmaeckers, J.E., Kessels, A.G. and Kleijnen, J. (1996). Analgesic efficacy and safety of paracetamol-codeine combinations versus paracetamol alone: a systematic review. *British Medical Journal*, **313**(7053), 321–325.

Cranney, A., Papaioannou, A., Zytaruk, N., Hanley, D., Adachi, J., Goltzman, D., Murray, T. and Hodsman, A. (2006). Parathyroid hormone for the treatment of osteoporosis: a systematic review. *Canadian Medical Association Journal*, **175**(1), 52–59.

Department of Health (DH) (2006). Improving Patients' Access to Medicines: A guide to implementing nurse and pharmacist independent prescribing within the NHS in England. Available at www.dh.gov.uk. Accessed 27.07.07.

Eckhardt, K., Li, S., Ammon, S., Schanzle, G., Mikus, G. and Eichelbaum, M. (1998). Same incidence of adverse drug events after codeine administration irrespective of the genetically-determined differences in morphine formation. *Pain*, **76**(1–2), 27–33.

Felsenberg, D., Miller, P., Armbrecht, G., Wilson, K., Schimmer, R.C. and Papapoulos, S.E. (2005). Oral ibandronic acid significantly reduces the risk of vertebral fractures of greater severity after 1, 2, and 3 years in post-menopausal women with osteoporosis. *Bone*, **37**(5), 651–654.

Freynhagen, R., Strojek, K., Griesing, T., Whalen, E. and Balkenohl, M. (2005). Efficacy of pregabalin in neuropathic pain evaluated in a 12-week, randomised, double-blind, multicentre, placebo-controlled trial of flexible and fixed-dose regimens. *Pain*, **115**(3), 254–263.

Furlan, A.D., Sandoval, J.A., Mailis-Gagnon, A. and Tunks, E. (2006). Opioids for chronic non-cancer pain: a meta-analysis of effectiveness and side effects. *Canadian Medical Association Journal*, **174**(11), 1589–1594.

Gotzsche, P.C. and Johansen, H.K. (2003). Short-term low-dose corticosteroids vs placebo and nonsteroidal anti-inflammatory drugs in rheumatoid arthritis (Cochrane Review). *The Cochrane Library*, **1**.

Health Professions Council (HPC) (2004). *Standards of Conduct, Performance and Ethics*. London: HPC.

Hollingshead, J., Duhmke, R.M. and Cornblath, D.R. (2006). Tramadol for neuropathic pain (Cochrane Review). *The Cochrane Library*, **3**.

Jones, G., Halbert, J., Crotty, M., Shanahan, E.M., Batterham, M. and Ahern, M. (2003). The effect of treatment on radiological progression in rheumatoid arthritis: a systematic review of randomized placebo-controlled trials. *Rheumatology*, **42**(1), 6–13.

Langford, R., McKenna, F., Ratcliffe, S., Vojtassak, J. and Richarz, U. (2006). Transdermal fentanyl for improvement of pain and functioning in osteoarthritis: a randomized, placebo-controlled trial. *Arthritis & Rheumatism*, 54(6), 1829–1837.

Levy, R.A., Vilela, V.S., Cataldo, M.J., Ramos, R.C., Duarte, J.L., Tura, B.R., Albuquerque, E.M. and Jesus, N.R. (2001). Hydroxychloroquine (HCQ) in lupus pregnancy: double-blind and placebo-controlled study. *Lupus*, **10**(6), 401–404.

Liberman, U.A., Hochberg, M.C., Geusens, P., Shah, A., Lin, J., Chattopadhyay, A. and Ross, P.D. (2006). Hip and non-spine fracture risk reductions differ among anti-resorptive agents: evidence from randomised controlled trials. *International Journal of Clinical Practice*, **60**(11),1394–1400.

Luqmani, R., Hennell, S., Estrach, C., Birrell, F., Bosworth, A., Davenport, G., Fokke, C., Goodson, N., Jeffreson, P., Lamb, E., Mohammed, R., Oliver, S., Stableford, Z., Walsh, D., Washbrook, C. and Webb, F. (2006). British Society for Rheumatology and British Health Professionals in Rheumatology Guideline for the Management of Rheumatoid Arthritis (the first two years). *Rheumatology* Advance Access 13 July, doi:10.1093/rheumatology/kel215b.

Madhok, R., Wu, O., McKellar, G. and Singh, G. (2006). Non-steroidal anti-inflammatory drugs: changes in prescribing may be warranted. *Rheumatology*, **45**(12), 1458–1460.

Mason, L., Moore, R.A., Derry, S., Edwards, J.E. and McQuay, H.J. (2004a). Systematic review of topical capsaicin for the treatment of chronic pain. *British Medical Journal*, **328**(7446), 991–994.

Mason, L., Moore, R.A., Edwards, J.E., Derry, S. and McQuay, H.J. (2004b). Topical NSAIDs for acute pain: a meta-analysis. *BMC Family Practice*, **5**(10), 5–10.

Maxwell, S. and Walley, T. (2002). Teaching safe and effective prescribing in UK medical schools. *British Medical Journal*, **324**(7353), 930–931.

McQuay, H.J., Carroll, D. and Glynn, C.J. (1992). Low dose amitriptyline in the treatment of chronic pain. *Anaesthesia*, **47**(8), 646–652.

Moore, A., Collins, S., Carroll, D. and McQuay, H. (1997). Paracetamol with and without codeine in acute pain: a quantitative systematic review. *Pain*, **70**(2–3), 193–201.

Nursing and Midwifery Council (NMC) (2006). Standards of Proficiency for Nurse and Midwife Prescribers. Available at www.nmc-uk.org. Accessed 27.07.07.

O'Dell, J.R., Leff, R., Paulsen, G., Haire, C., Mallek, J., Eckhoff, P.J., Fernandez, A., Blakely, K., Wees, S., Stoner, J., Hadley, S., Felt, J., Palmer, W., Waytz, P., Churchill, M., Klassen, L. and Moore, G. (2002). Treatment of rheumatoid arthritis with methotrexate and hydroxychloroquine, methotrexate and sulfasalazine, or a combination of the three medications: results of a two-year, randomized, double-blind, placebo-controlled trial. *Arthritis & Rheumatism*, **46**(5), 1164–1170.

Osiri, M., Shea, B., Robinson, V., Suarez-Almazor, M., Strand, V., Tugwell, P. and Wells, G. (2003). Leflunomide for the treatment of rheumatoid arthritis: a systematic review and metaanalysis. *Journal of Rheumatology*, **30**(6), 1182–1190.

Pheasant, H., Bursk, A., Goldfarb, J., Azen, S.P., Weiss, J.N. and Borelli, L. (1983). Amitriptyline and chronic low-back pain. A randomized double-blind crossover study. *Spine*, **8**(5), 552–557.

Raskin, J., Pritchett, Y.L., Wang, F., D'Souza, D.N., Waninger, A.L., Iyengar, S. and Wernicke, J.F. (2005). A double-blind, randomized multicenter trial comparing duloxetine with placebo in the management of diabetic peripheral neuropathic pain. *Pain Medicine*, **6**(5), 346–356.

van Riel, P.L., Taggart, A.J., Sany, J., Gaubitz, M., Nab, H.W., Pedersen, R., Freundlich, B. and MacPeek, D. (2006). Efficacy and safety of combination etanercept and methotrexate versus etanercept alone in patients with rheumatoid arthritis with an inadequate response to methotrexate: the ADORE study. *Annals of the Rheumatic Diseases*, **65**(11), 1478–1483.

Royal College of Physicians (RCP) (2000). Principles of pain control in palliative care for adults. Guidance prepared by a Working Group of the Ethical Issues in Medicine Committee of the Royal College of Physicians. *Journal of the Royal College of Physicians of London*, **34**(4), 350–352.

Royal College of Physicians (RCP) (2002). *Glucocorticoid-induced Osteoporosis*. London: RCP.

Royal Pharmaceutical Society of Great Britain (RPSGB) (2006). *Medicines, Ethics and Practice: A guide for pharmacists*. London: Pharmaceutical Press.

Saarto, T. and Wiffen, P.J. (2005). Anti-depressants for neuropathic pain (Cochrane Review). *The Cochrane Library*, **3**.

Schlesinger, N., Schumacher, R., Catton, M. and Maxwell, L. (2006). Colchicine for acute gout (Cochrane Review). *The Cochrane Library*, **4**.

Schumacher, H.R. Jr, Boice, J.A., Daikh, D.I., Mukhopadhyay, S., Malmstrom, K., Ng, J., Tate, G.A. and Molina, J. (2002). Randomised double-blind trial of etoricoxib and indometacin in treatment of acute gouty arthritis. *British Medical Journal*, **324**(7352), 1488–1492.

Seeman, E., Crans, G.G., Diez-Perez, A., Pinette, K.V. and Delmas, P.D. (2006). Anti-vertebral fracture efficacy of raloxifene: a meta-analysis. *Osteoporosis International*, **17**(2), 313–316.

Shea, B., Wells, G., Cranney, A., Zytaruk, N., Robinson, V., Griffith, L., Ortiz, Z., Peterson, J., Adachi, J., Tugwell, P. and Guyatt, G. (2002). Meta-analyses of therapies for post-menopausal osteoporosis VII: Meta-analysis of calcium supplementation for the prevention of post-menopausal osteoporosis. *Endocrine Reviews*, **23**(4), 552–559.

Sorge, J. and Sittl, R. (2004). Transdermal buprenorphine in the treatment of chronic pain: results of a phase III, multicenter, randomized, double-blind, placebo-controlled study. *Clinical Therapeutics*, **26**(11), 1808–1820.

Stevenson, M., Davis, S., Lloyd-Jones, M. and Beverley, C. (2007). The clinical effectiveness and cost-effectiveness of strontium ranelate for the prevention of osteoporotic fragility fractures in post-menopausal women. *Health Technology Assessment*, **11**(4), 1–134.

Suarez-Almazor, M.E., Belseck, E., Shea, B., Homik, J., Wells, G. and Tugwell, P. (2000a). Anti-malarials for treating rheumatoid arthritis (Cochrane Review). *The Cochrane Library*, **4**.

Suarez-Almazor, M.E., Belseck, E., Shea, B., Wells, G. and Tugwell, P. (2000b). Methotrexate for rheumatoid arthritis (Cochrane Review). *The Cochrane Library*, **2**.

Suarez-Almazor, M.E., Belseck, E., Shea, B., Wells, G. and Tugwell, P. (2000c) Sulfasalazine for rheumatoid arthritis (Cochrane Review). *The Cochrane Library*, **2**.

van der Veen, M.J. and Bijlsma, J.W. (1993). The effect of methylprednisolone pulse therapy on methotrexate treatment of rheumatoid arthritis. *Clinical Rheumatology*, **12**(4), 500–505.

van Tulder, M.W., Scholten, R.J., Koes, B.W. and Deyo, R.A. (2000) Nonsteroidal anti-inflammatory drugs for low back pain: a systematic review within the framework of the Cochrane Collaboration Back Review Group. *Spine*, **25**(19), 2501–2513.

Whiting, B., Holford, N. and Begg, E. (2002). Clinical Pharmacology: Principles and practice of drug therapy in medical education. *British Journal of Clinical Pharmacology*, **54**(1), 1–2.

Wiffen, P.J., McQuay, H.J., Edwards, J.E. and Moore, R.A. (2005). Gabapentin for acute and chronic pain (Cochrane Review). *The Cochrane Library*, **3**.

Williams, H.J., Egger, M.J., Singer, J.Z., Willkens, R.F., Kalunian, K.C., Clegg, D.O., Skosey, J.L., Brooks, R.H., Alarcon, G.S. and Steen, V.D. (1994). Comparison of hydroxychloroquine and placebo in the treatment of the arthropathy of mild systemic lupus erythematosus. *Journal of Rheumatology*, **21**(8), 1457–1462.

Woolacott, N.F., Khadjesari, Z.C., Bruce, I.N. and Riemsma, R.P. (2006). Etanercept and infliximab for the treatment of psoriatic arthritis: a systematic review. *Clinical and Experimental Rheumatology*, **24**(5), 587–593.

Zhang, W., Doherty, M., Bardin, T., Pascual, E., Barskova, V., Conaghan, P., Gerster, J., Jacobs, J., Leeb, B., Liote, F., McCarthy, G., Netter, P., Nuki, G., Perez-Ruiz, F., Pignone, A., Pimentao, J., Punzi, L., Roddy, E., Uhlig, T. and Zimmermann-

Gorska, I. (2006). EULAR evidence-based recommendations for gout. Part II: Management: Report of a task force of the EULAR Standing Committee for International Clinical Studies Including Therapeutics (ESCISIT). *Annals of the Rheumatic Diseases*, **65**(10), 1312–1324.

Zhang, W., Jones, A. and Doherty, M. (2004). Does paracetamol (acetaminophen) reduce the pain of osteoarthritis? A meta-analysis of randomised controlled trials. *Annals of the Rheumatic Diseases*, **63**(8), 901–907.

Zochling, J., van der Heijde, H.D., Dougados, M. and Braun, J. (2006). Current evidence for the management of ankylosing spondylitis: a systematic literature review for the ASAS/EULAR management recommendations in ankylosing spondylitis. *Annals of the Rheumatic Diseases*, **65**(4), 423–432.